PUPPIES, LAMBS, BUNNIES & MOTORCYCLES

A childhood memoir about hard work
and achieving your dreams.

—

SECOND EDITION

BY DWIGHT B. HINKEL

PUPPIES, LAMBS, BUNNIES & MOTORCYCLES is a childhood memoir. The events, locations, dates, names and conversations in this book, while intended to be true, are recreated from the author's memory. The accuracy of the information provided is a priority, however, it is not guaranteed.

Proofreading by Sheila Hinkel, Marvel Bailey, Scott Ulm and Fred Renner
Design, Copyediting and Self-Publishing Services by Breanna Thompson

FOR RAY AND ELMA,
WHO PUT UP WITH ME
FOR OVER EIGHTEEN YEARS—

CONTENTS

PROLOGUE

I had been waiting every day of my life for this moment. The suspense was killing me. At thirteen-years-old, I was about to fire up my project from the last three years. In a barn, I'd found a 1948 Royal Enfield Bullet 500 motorcycle in boxes. After reading *Modern Motorcycle Mechanics* by J.B. Nicholson multiple times, I had spent countless hours rebuilding the engine, painting, creating various cables for the clutch, throttle, choke, spark advance, and front brake. I was now ready for the moment of truth.

I had gone through the procedure hundreds of times in my mind:

(1) open the fuel petcocks located under the colossal chrome gas tank,

(2) tickle the Amal carburetor until gasoline runs all over the new paint,

(3) apply the choke,

(4) retard the manual spark advance to prevent a broken leg,

(5) work the kick-starter until the engine is coming up on compression, and

(6) with all of my one-hundred pounds of brawn, straighten my right leg while jumping on the kick-starter.

The mighty single ticked over and...

CHAPTER 1
UNCLE ART

My total infatuation with motorcycles was all my uncle's fault. My Dad's older, bachelor-brother, Arthur, had returned from Europe after serving as a Demolition Engineer for the United States Army during World War II. The oldest of eleven siblings, tall, with black hair and piercing grey-green eyes, full of wisdom and ambition, he moved back to the family farm south of Arena, North Dakota. The talents he acquired in the military seemed to make him superhuman. He could overhaul anything mechanical. He even bought a turning lathe to craft parts and would turn commutators on starters and generators. He could rewind electric motors, plumb a house, fix a broken pump jack, or custom engineer a better farm implement. He had purchased an acetylene gas torch, fueled by calcium carbide, and an electric arc welder. He was the best welder I ever knew. His overhead welds were works of art, worthy of exhibition in The Guggenheim. With his skills, tools and super-friendly disposition, Art was loved and respected by all. The local neighbors and some not-so-local would bring their broken items to him to fix. They always went home happy.

Art, or for those of us with better manners, "Uncle Art," had first enamored himself to his nephews and nieces by building a complete outdoor gym. Handmade and painted in bright colors, the set consisted of a merry-go-round, a slide, and a teeter-totter with a unique feature—an *adjustable fulcrum*. Since the clan of cousins varied greatly in age and weight, having an easily adjustable fulcrum made it possible for kids of different sizes to balance! Ingenious for 1954!

My Dad, Raymond, was two years younger than Art. Dad revered his older brother and tried to emulate him. Our farm was one-and-a-half miles north of the old homestead (where Art lived). At that location, their family had struggled to get through The Great Depression. Desperately poor, my grandfather's love of anything fermented compounded the dire situation. Even though they were living on a farm, with thirteen mouths to feed, food was in short supply. Their tough upbringing occasionally showed in their lack of compassion. Art returned from the war with optimism and knowledge that was infectious and helped the whole family shape a new vision that sustained them for the rest of their lives.

It was around 1957. It was a beautiful, bright North Dakota summer day. There was sunshine, fresh air and the birds were singing. It was a day to enjoy. I was scavenging the farm for enough BBs to take my new Daisy air rifle hunting.

An unusual sound broke the serenity. A small series of explosions were increasing in volume and getting closer to the house. It was the sound only a Harley-Davidson can make.

Our family ran out onto the porch and stared down the driveway.

"IT'S UNCLE ART ON A MOTORCYCLE!" I exclaimed.

He came chugging up to the house, astride his mechanical marvel. He looked like a knight ready to slay the dragon.

It was a Harley-Davidson 45 flathead. It had a big hand shifter, foot clutch, giant kick-starter, mechanical doodads, and gewgaws everywhere. Smoke and fumes seemed to emanate from every engine seam. As the beast stopped, a puddle of oil began forming under the engine. We could feel the heat radiating from twenty feet away. The smell of unburned hydrocarbons permeated the air. Raw gas, burnt oil, and exhaust filled our nostrils with an aroma that cannot be described for those never experiencing it. As a seven-year-old, I took it all in. I was hooked.

Art beamed with pride atop his steed.

"Would you like a ride?" Art asked my dad.

"Of course," my father replied.

My Mom, Elma, looked on as if Dad had just volunteered for D-Day.

The beast started on the first kick, and Dad and Art went chugging down the driveway. While they were away, I asked Mom, "Will I get a ride too?"

My mother's face turned to a look of horror. The specter of losing her husband and son on the same day shook her deep religious convictions.

"You'll have to ask your father IF he makes it back," she replied.

She looked at me as if it was the last time she would see me alive, turned, and sulked into the house. There I stood alone in the sunlight, smelling the breeze and listening to the distant, pulsating sound of the big, v-twin engine. As the sound drew nearer, my anticipation of pleasure grew and grew.

I was going to get a ride on Uncle Art's motorcycle! Surely, I must be the luckiest kid in the whole world!

Art and my Dad pulled up in front of the house. Art shut down the beast. They chattered hysterically. Tears streamed down their red faces, flushed from the wind. They laughed as only brothers can laugh. A cacophony of smells added to the excitement.

Now, it was my turn!

"Uncle Art, can I have a ride, too?" I blurted out.

"If it's OK with your Dad," Art replied.

Somehow, children possess the trait of recognizing when adults' responses are less than authentic. My Dad looked at me with what must have been the same look on Abraham's face when he was asked by God to sacrifice his son. My Dad started stammering, but Art offered to make it a short, slow ride, just down the driveway and back. My Dad nervously accepted. Art began going through the ritual to start the beast.

In the eyes of a seven-year-old, it was akin to watching Merlin cast a spell. Several years before, we bought our first television and watched Disney's

Fantasia. Now, "The Sorcerer's Apprentice" scenes co-mingled in my mind with those of Uncle Art. To be the Sorcerer, all Art needed was a wizard cap, a robe and a list of incantations.

Art rose up on the kick-starter and jumped down with all his might.

"Chuff."

Kick the kick-starter to compression, and repeat.

"Chuff."

Repeat.

"Chuff."

Repeat.

"Chuff."

This process went on for several minutes. I heard Art mumbling the Sorcerer's secret incantations under his breath. They were too garbled to decipher, but from what I could tell, he was summoning ancient powers. I heard multiple references to God, Jesus, and other deities. These were powerful words not meant for my ears. I'd try to remember these incantations to help me cast spells of my own in the future.

Art had kicked the machine until he couldn't breathe. As my father took over kicking duties, Art's tongue hung from his mouth. A freshly lit Camel cigarette dangled from under his upper lip. When the smoke curled up from the cigarette, Art would cock his head to one side to avoid getting it in his eyes. After several minutes, my Dad relinquished the kick-starting duties to Art and Dad lit up a Lucky Strike of his own. They didn't realize it at the time, but the cigarette habit would eventually kill them both. They worked in shifts, jumping on the kick-starter for about ten minutes. The beast had somehow died right before my ride. This pattern seemed to be a trend throughout my life. The near realization of mortal pleasure, only to be crushed by some unforeseen event.

Because he started his smoking habit at the ripe age of six, Art was spent from all the kicking. Thirty-four years of smoking had taken its toll on his stamina. His blue tongue was hanging from his mouth, he was coughing, and his hand was unsteady as he lit up another Camel.

"The plugs are fouled," he wheezed. "Do you have a plug wrench?"

Minutes later, the fouled plugs were lying on the porch steps while Dad heated the ends with a propane torch. With dry spark plugs, the Harley burst to life on the first kick.

Now, it was MY turn for a ride.

"It's getting late. I better go," Art hollered out over the noise of the engine. "I'll have to give you a ride another time."

I was devastated as Art chugged away. A perfect day ruined by something called "spark plugs." I've hated them ever since. Even mention of the name "Champion" rouses me to feelings of anger.

Why is it that things offered, and then denied, are those most desired by our souls? It's like when I go to a car dealership, and the car I want to buy is sold two minutes before my offer! I've concluded there must be a cosmic connection.

I didn't get a ride that day, but the events forever changed me. I was hooked on motorcycles for the rest of my life. They spurred my love of all things mechanical, chartered a course for me to graduate college with a Mechanical Engineering degree, and supplied me with enough Sorcerer's incantations to get me through rough times.

CHAPTER 2
BIG RED

The disappointment of not getting a ride on Art's motorcycle started me thinking. *Could I cobble together something with an engine and two wheels?*

Around 1953, my blonde, lanky, tomboy, older sister, Shirley, saved up enough money and purchased herself a black, French, three-speed, boys' bicycle. It was a great bike. No dérailleurs to break, it used a three-speed planetary drive. It had skinny tires, a nicely sprung seat, and perfectly-spaced gears. Before seeing Art's motorcycle, it was the bike I had aspired to own.

Shirley was eight years older than me, so by the time I was eight, she was sixteen and had already graduated to cars. I adopted her bike and rode it many miles. It never let me down. I did manage to tip over in the gravel several times, but that's another story. As far as bicycles go, I felt Shirley's bike was too new and fancy to try to modify into a motorbike.

My next oldest sibling, Sharon, was six years my senior. More of a homemaker than Shirley, she had red-brown pigtails, big blue eyes, freckles, and suffered from all the maladies middle children possess. She owned a discarded bicycle that might lend itself well to modification.

She was always trying to play catch-up to Shirley. She had no money, but when Shirley got her bike, Sharon wanted one as well. After badgering my parents for weeks, Dad decided to put the matter to rest by buying Sharon a bike. We were dirt poor, so a bike, even a crappy one, would be a major purchase. Dad had many great attributes, not among them was shopping. His first thought was always, "What's the cheapest solution with the least effort?" In this case, the solution to buying Sharon a bike was to visit The Bismarck Trading Post, a second-hand store in Bismarck, North Dakota.

On a shopping trip to get farm supplies, we stopped at The Trading Post. Across from the World War Memorial Building on Fifth Street, Dad and I entered the familiar store with high hopes. The store had an odd odor all its own. The smell of mold, dust, oil, soldering flux, and dated electrical wiring (with a hint of smoke thrown in for extra flavor), permeated the store. In amongst the old washing machines, refrigerators, lawnmowers, and engine parts, my Dad struck gold. There it was! A faded, red girls' bike with balloon tires so big they looked like they came off of a piece of earthmoving equipment. Complete, single-speed and probably cheap, Dad had found the bicycle of his dreams.

Trying to look disinterested, my Dad said, "Are you selling the bike?"

The store owner, Roger, apparently had Dale Carnegie training and replied, "Depends."

The game was on. New bikes at the time were about fifteen dollars. The store owner went into a routine suitable for a vacuum cleaner salesman. He pointed out the "almost-like-new" tires, the little wear on the pedals and hand grips, and what looked like a new chain. He dream-built with my father about how Sharon would scream with delight at the sight of her nearly-new bike.

He wanted eight dollars. Dad countered by pointing out the scratch on the fender and the scuff mark on the handlebars. He eventually agreed to pay five dollars. He grinned ear-to-ear as we left the store. *What a steal! Only five dollars for an "almost new" bike? Sharon would be ecstatic!*

As I helped Dad load the bike into the trunk of our car, a 1956 Studebaker President, I noticed the bike seemed to have a rather substantial gravitational pull. I had ridden Shirley's French racer many times and was accustomed to its weight. The heft of Sharon's bike seemed much more formidable.

There is an adage about locking up your bicycle to prevent it from theft:

> "All bikes weigh seventy pounds. If you have a twenty-pound bike, you need a fifty-pound chain. If you have a thirty-pound bike, you need a forty-pound chain. If you have a sixty-pound bike, you need a ten-pound chain. Seventy-pound bikes don't need chains because no one will steal them."

Sharon's new bike was of the seventy-plus pound category.

We got home with the bike just as my sisters got back from Mrs. McDonough's music lessons in Wing. While Dad and I unloaded "Big Red," Shirley mounted her French racer. Dad proudly pointed out the attributes of the *almost new* machine to Sharon, handed her the handlebars and wished her well. Shirley came up on her three-speed and expected Sharon to pull alongside. Sharon stepped into the bike, leveled the handlebars, positioned the pedals, and placed her full body weight on the right pedal. The bike barely moved. As she transferred her weight to the other pedal, the bike imperceptibly picked up speed.

Meanwhile, Shirley had pedaled up and down the driveway several times, waiting for Sharon to catch up. As Sharon pedaled with all her might, she finally got to the end of our eighth-mile drive. She turned around and came back. The return was slightly downhill. She was picking up speed. As she approached the starting point, a smile appeared on her face. Dad had shown her how to use the coaster brakes by peddling backward. She started to apply the brakes. With the slightest tap, the rear wheel locked, sending the bike into an uncontrollable skid on the gravel. With the enormous mass of the machine now in a skid, Sharon lost control, going down in a cloud of dirt and dust, skinning her ankle and elbow.

Roger, the salesman, had been correct. Sharon would scream, but not in delight. Crying and bloodied, she got up and ran into the house. My Dad spoke a few Sorcerer incantations, and then started nervously laughing. I felt awful for Sharon. I picked up the bike and tried to pedal away. I failed. I wasn't even heavy enough to make the pedal move!

Sharon tried riding the bike several more times before it was parked permanently behind the farm shop. She had been humiliated by everyone else that had modern, lightweight bikes rather than one more suited for military use. Little did I know at the time, the challenges and excitement that "Big Red" would provide me in the future. It would become the motorcycle of my dreams.

CHAPTER 3
DESIGN LOGIC

The dream of riding a motorcycle became an obsession. I fantasized about how a poor farm boy like me could afford to buy one. I got to work.

I sold garden seeds in the spring and Christmas cards in the fall. I saved my allowance and birthday money. When she could afford it, my mother gave me twenty-five cents a week for allowance. As my nest egg approached twenty dollars, I started shopping.

I intently read *Popular Mechanics* and *Popular Science* magazines that had been discarded by our church pastor. I still read them today; thankfully, they aren't his twenty-year-old moldy rags.

After sixty years of reading them, I've noticed that a repeating dream of the writers is and always has been—*flying cars*. Every year or so, an article is published describing how they are the next big thing and how the trend is about to take the nation by storm. It's never happened. I doubt it ever will.

I suppose if you live in a big city, the thought of flying over congested freeways is appealing. However, growing up in rural North Dakota, I've never seen the logic. To me, something that's marginally safe at ground level seems exponentially less safe at tens of thousands of feet above the ground. With all the recalls made by automobile companies, I wouldn't have great faith in a Yugo or Pinto auto-airplane.

Even though I wasn't very interested in the articles promoting flying cars, the magazines did contain abundant advertisements for desired bikes, Cushman scooters, Clinton two-stroke engines, Harley-Davidson, and other mechanical inventions and products appealing to a nine-year-old boy, or a ninety-year-old man. To my dismay, there were *zero* options in the twenty-dollar range that could launch me into being a motorcycle owner. While riding the school bus one day, an idea popped into my head.

Big Red could be a motorbike!

Leftover from a gas-powered washing machine, we had a Briggs and Stratton WMB 1/2-horsepower engine lying in the corner of the shop. It was a relic from before rural electrification during the 1950s when many families switched from washing machines that used gasoline-powered engines to ones that ran on electricity. It was perfect! It even had a built-in kick-starter and a v-belt pulley drive! My Dad had let me disassemble and reassemble the engine as part of my second-grade education. I knew the engine inside and out and had scars from accidentally touching the hot exhaust while it was running.

Now, how to mount the engine to Big Red?

Slowly a plan evolved in my undeveloped nine-year-old brain. Since it was a girls' bike, Big Red did not have a top tube; it was a step-through. I could mount the engine in the step-through portion of the frame. After welding a rectangular piece of steel to the frame above the pedals, the engine was mounted in place, just like the pictures I'd seen of old motorcycles.

Now how do I get the half horsepower from the engine to the rear wheels? I had already learned about pulley ratios in my 4-H club, so I knew I needed to attach a big v-belt pulley to the rear wheel.

Farm junk piles are amazing places. They were the early Amazon of parts shopping for poor farmers. Our junk pile must have been "Junk Pile Prime." It had *everything* including old cars, engines, discarded farm implements, and pieces of steel. They were all in abundance and available the same day! Digging through some abandoned, rusty combine parts, I found a pulley that was about fifteen inches in diameter. The pulley would be perfect to attach to Big Red's rear wheel. I removed the bicycle's rear wheel, drilled the appropriate holes in the pulley, and affixed the pulley to the spokes of the rear wheel with wire. After reinstalling the rear wheel, all I needed was a v-belt of the appropriate length. I used three dollars of my nest egg to buy the belt at our local Farmers Union.

As I tried to install the v-belt, I faced a serious design problem. A bicycle chain goes above, and below, the frame of a bike. If you've ever removed one, you know the chain splits by removing a connector link. V-belts are continuous and have no connector. I needed a creative solution to get the belt installed. At this point, I resorted to some of my Uncle Art's incantations. They didn't work. I guess Sorcerer's genes don't run deep. I would have to figure out how to get the v-belt across the frame of the bike without cutting the belt, and without the use of the paranormal. After several days, a solution came to me.

If I can't cut the belt, why not cut the frame and weld it back together?

Our farm's Forney electric arc welder and a hacksaw made quick work of cutting the bike frame. An hour later with the belt in place, my Dad had re-welded the frame. He helped me align the belt with the engine pulley, drill mounting holes in the engine-mounting plate we had welded to the frame, and bolt the engine into position. We left the bicycle pedals in place. I closed the choke and pedaled away. Being a coaster bike the pedals didn't turn when coasting, and by leaving them on the bike, I had brakes by pedaling backward. *I was ready to ride!*

The engine sputtered to life, and I was off. I had rigged a push-pull wire from an old lawnmower to the carburetor as a throttle. The engine needed to run at full throttle to generate enough power to propel the bike. After driving for a few minutes, I returned to the shop with the realization I had no method of disengaging the engine from driving the bike. In other words, the idea of a clutch had escaped my design logic. At ten miles per hour, the shop loomed closer. I panicked and pedaled backward, engaging the brakes. Thank God the brakes were still catchy, because they locked up, stopping the engine and the bike. My first ride had ended safely, but I knew some redesign was needed. I had to find a clutch.

After some more reading in old magazines, I discovered that Whizzer motorbikes used something called a "centrifugal clutch." This wonderful device would disengage at slow engine speeds but would engage as the engine was throttled-up. I wrote a letter to the Whizzer factory to inquire about acquiring a clutch. The Whizzer factory had ceased production some years earlier, but parts were still available. A Whizzer clutch was about ten dollars but was not available in the shaft diameter I needed for my engine. Another plan for a clutch was required.

Harvest season was upon us, and I needed to put aside Big Red while helping my father harvest. Today he'd most likely be arrested for using a nine-year-old to drive a truck hauling grain, but in 1959 it was not unusual for children to help with the annual harvest. Luckily, I was tall for my age, so, I could use the standard pedals of our Studebaker truck.

My father would combine until the hopper was full of grain, and then he would motion for me to drive the truck under the combine's unloading auger. Driving close enough to the combine would not be complicated *if* we were working on a flat, paved, parking lot, but we were harvesting on hilly ground, strewn with rocks and dead furrows. As the truck approached the combine, Dad would start motioning furiously with his arms and Sorcerer's incantations would spew from his mouth. His wild gyrations reminded me of a person on fire trying to beat out the flames with their hands. I was a good student, but apparently, I had missed the semaphore classes. I had no clue as to what my Dad was trying to communicate. As I drove closer, I could see the veins bulging in his neck and forehead. I perceived I was doing something wrong. I drove within inches of the combine and parked the truck box directly under the grain auger.

I jumped out of the cab and asked my Dad what was wrong. He said I had done it all wrong, but somehow my driving had turned out okay! Over the next ten years, this process would repeat itself hundreds of times. In Dad's eyes, I never quite got it right, but I never accidentally drove the truck into the combine, either. Thinking about the situation today, as a parent myself, I realize Dad was just overly-protective... of the combine.

During one of those combine-truck encounters, I had parked directly across from the combine's auger drive system. The auger clutch was a simple v-belt drive with a belt tensioner. There it was, right in front of me, the CLUTCH SOLUTION!

A simple belt tensioner would work as a clutch on Big Red!

CHAPTER 4
LET THERE BE LIGHT

The simple belt tensioner with an idler pulley worked perfectly. I did have to invest another three dollars for a longer belt, but now I had a working clutch to disengage the engine from the rear wheel when stopping. I could also start the engine without needing the rear wheel spinning. Although the system required me to have one hand on the belt tensioner while driving the bike, it worked rather well for a total investment of six dollars. With fourteen dollars still in my nest egg, I decided to splurge.

The *Sears, Roebuck and Co.* catalog was never more than a hole away in our three-hole outhouse. Thumbing through the bicycle section, which was luckily still intact, and then opening the door for better lighting, I struck GOLD! The bicycle section was full of accessories perfect for my project. Fancy handlebar grips with red, green, blue, white, and yellow plastic tassels, just like I had seen advertised on authentic Indian motorcycles, peaked my interest.

A bicycle headlight (lit by a miniature generator), would be required for safety. A pair of black engineer's boots were needed to protect my feet and shins from the gravel roads. And finally, a cap, just like the one Marlon Brando wore in *The Wild One* would top it all off. Twelve dollars plus postage and two weeks of waiting would reward me with the PERFECT combination of style and practicality.

When my merchandise arrived, the boots fit well, better than any shoes I had ever owned. Putting on the mail-order cap and looking at myself in the mirror, I was the original "Mini-Me," a smaller, replica version of Brando.

"Now, I'm a REAL biker," I thought.

The multi-colored, plastic, handlebar-grip tassels looked great dangling in the sunshine until I started driving. The tassels were about twelve inches long, and as I took off, they came in contact with the hot engine of the mighty Briggs and Stratton. Soon, six inches of tassel melted off each end of the streamers. The remaining tassels looked as if they had been through a fire. Curling from the heat, and becoming stiff, blackened nubs, they stuck out from the ends of the handlebar grips, resembling colored toothbrush handles more than tassels. Eventually, I cut off the tassels' mangled remnants, neutering Big Red. Apparently, the advertisements in the *Sears* catalog had been misleading.

Bastard admen!

As the melted plastic on the engine turned to smoke and rose into my eyes and nostrils, I contemplated what project to work on next.

Fall was fast-approaching. As the daylight grew shorter, mounting the headlight would be required to safely drive to my 4-H club once a month and our church Youth League every Wednesday night. After installing the headlight on the handlebars, the miniature generator was attached to the front fork of the frame, next to the tire. A spring-loaded mechanism engaged a knurled wheel to rub against the tire. As the front wheel turned, the generator turned, sending electricity up through a wire to the handlebar-mounted headlight. A man wouldn't walk on the moon for another ten years, flying cars weren't yet in production, but I had a generator-powered bicycle light? *We were living in an age of wonder!*

As soon as dusk settled in, I decided to test the headlight by driving the half-mile to my cousin Larry Buller's farm. They were as poor as we were, so there was no caste system to overcome. Larry was was two years my senior and was tall for his age. He was amazingly ambitious and inventive. He even made a pinball machine from plywood and old parts! I idolized him. He was smart and grew up to be a jet pilot. As I drove to Larry's, I engaged the generator. A dim light illuminated my path. As Big Red gained speed, the light got brighter and brighter. It was more than adequate. As I turned around in Larry's yard and returned home, I was smug in my nine-year-old genius. The Bible says, "Pride Goeth before the Fall." The Bible was right.

The next night was church Youth League. As Big Red and I hummed our way to the church (about a mile and a half from our farm), the world seemed in perfect order. Bugs were hitting me in the face, burning remnants of plastic tassels permeated the air, and the cool autumn breeze brought tears to my eyes. All was well with my soul.

I didn't need the headlight on the way to church, but on the trip home, the sun had set, and the landscape had turned inky black. If "The Sorcerer's Apprentice" had caused my imagination to work overtime, now scenes of the Headless Horseman from *The Legend of Sleepy Hollow* danced in my brain. A variety of wild animals inhabited this rural land including eagles, owls, deer, coyotes, bobcats, and the occasional mountain lion. I would feel more secure as soon as I was back at home. Even though I was now a "biker" at heart, my brain still belonged to a nine-year-old kid. I was scared of the dark.

Thankfully the Briggs started, and I was off. Engaging the generator rewarded me with a warm yellow light. The light and generator were designed for an ordinary single-speed pedal bicycle, that on its best day, would not go much faster than fifteen miles per hour. Approximately a half-mile from the church, Big Red was approaching its top speed of about twenty miles per hour. The light was getting brighter and brighter, until I imagined I was looking into the sun, and then, "*P-O-P!*"

The headlight burned out.

After the flash, I had no night vision. I couldn't see a thing. I felt the front wheel hit the gravel ridge and I lost control, launching me into the ditch beside the road. Big Red landed nearby. I walked over and looked, thankful it was unscathed (or so it appeared). I pushed Big Red back onto the road, and it restarted. I managed to get home by the light of the Milky Way. When I walked into the house, my Mom looked horrified to see me.

"Dwight, what happened?!"

I looked down and saw the torn shirt and pants. Blood was running down my arm and leg.

"Nothing," I replied, as I limped off to my room.

"Bitchin'!" I thought to myself. *"I really am a biker."*

CHAPTER 5
BESIDE MYSELF

The daylight hours grew shorter as we approached the Thanksgiving holiday. I decided to take one more ride on Big Red before winter. Somehow, the bike was softer to ride, and the handling felt strange. As I roared out of the corner at five miles per hour and lined up to make the turn into Larry's yard, the bike had stopped responding to my input. Suddenly, I found my feet on the ground, and I was running into the ditch behind the front wheel. With the handlebars in my grasp, the engine and the rear of the bike sailed past my ear.

Big Red had split into two parts. It was broken at the point where the frame tubes attached to the pedal crank housing. The only thing that had been holding Big Red together was the engine plate installed by my father. My off-road adventure when coming home from church had cracked the remaining welds.

Sadly, Big Red was parked behind Buller's machine shed. Now he was neutered and dead.

CHAPTER 6
THE FIND

The year was 1960. Thanksgiving was a family affair. We were invited to Wilton, North Dakota to break bread with my Dad's sister, Marvel, and her new husband, Richard. My Dad's sisters were all intelligent, and Aunt Marvel was no exception. She had married well; Uncle Richard was a keeper. As the mashed potatoes and turkey gravy were being passed around for the second time, I was still grieving over the loss of Big Red. After homemade pumpkin pie topped with whipped cream for dessert, our belt buckles strained to contain our meals and the men excused themselves to the outdoors.

It was a pleasant autumn day. As my Dad lit up a Lucky, Richard tried to make small talk with "Mini-Me." He asked what I had done with my summer vacation.

Richard was a genius. He worked for the North Dakota Department of Transportation as an Engineer, designing the traffic light systems for the state's highways.

I told him the tale of Big Red. With a wry smile, he said *he* used to ride a motorcycle, and *he still owned it*. My "biker" persona melted away, and I again became a nine-year-old boy.

"Gee whiz, can I see it?" I asked.

"Sure," he replied.

He led us to a small horse barn next to the house.

He opened the barn door and smells, not unlike those found in The Bismarck Trading Post, graced my nostrils. As my eyes adjusted to the light, I saw a black motorcycle frame leaning against the wall, and half-a-dozen boxes filled with parts stacked around it.

It was a 1948 Royal Enfield Bullet 500. Royal Canadian Mounted Police had ridden it from British Columbia, Canada, to Minot, North Dakota. There it was abandoned after breaking an engine-connecting rod. It became North Dakota State Property, where Richard bought it at a government auction. At this point, all the stars in the cosmos aligned, and after asking around, Richard found out about John Bernard Nicholson of Saskatoon, Saskatchewan, Canada, only a few hundred miles from the North Dakota border.

Nicholson Brothers Motorcycles was the premier provider of parts and manuals for all things related to British motorcycles. In 1942, J. B. Nicholson wrote the book *Modern Motorcycle Mechanics* (still in print), which outlined in great detail how to work on them, including the Royal Enfield Bullet. Richard had bought a new rod from Nicholson Bros., along with the book, and rebuilt the motorcycle.

Richard and Marvel had dated on the Enfield, until

it detonated the rod a second time, this time breaking the flywheel housing. After tearing down the engine and discovering the fractured engine case, Richard decided to park the motorcycle and get on with starting a family. It had remained in the barn ever since the tear-down, some three or four years earlier.

I had observed my Dad's negotiating skills and brought them to full use.

"Uncle Richard, would ya' sell it?" I asked.

"I don't think it's worth much," he replied.

"How much?" I asked.

"Thirty-five dollars," he replied.

The price sounded appropriate.

"I'll buy it as soon as I have the money."

"Okay," he said.

In true salesmanship fashion, we shook hands. My Dad looked at me dumbfounded as if I had put our farm's financial future at risk. I'm sure he considered my recent crash of Big Red as a precursor to insanity. Dad's assumption was only partially correct.

CHAPTER 7
FINANCIER

How long would it take to get thirty-five dollars to buy the Enfield? I mulled it over in my brain for a few days. A plan evolved. Christmas card season was coming up, and I could make ten dollars selling cards. I still had two dollars of my twenty dollar nest egg. I would make another ten dollars selling garden seeds next spring. Between now and next spring was about twenty-five weeks. At twenty-five cents a week for allowance, that was another six dollars and twenty-five cents. I was still short. Plus, I would need money for parts.

Luck is a fickle thing. Between my tragedies, I have always been fortunate enough to have strokes of good luck. My good luck was about to strike.

I had parked Big Red at Larry's farm after the "Parting-of-the-Red-Seam" incident (aptly named with my religious upbringing). Shortly after making the offer to Uncle Richard, Larry called.

"Hey cousin, would you like to sell Big Red?"

"Sure."

My Dale Carnegie senses snapped to attention.

"How much do you want?" he asked.

"Thirty-five dollars," I replied.

"I just sold my 4-H lamb, and I only have twenty-five," he said.

After a silence that would have made any used car salesman proud, I said, "Okay."

An investment of twenty bucks into Big Red had turned into twenty-five. WOW! The power of free enterprise!

We were thick into the Christmas season, and card sales were good. With that money, the money from Larry, my allowance, and my remaining nest egg, I had enough money to complete the purchase before Christmas!

The Enfield was waiting for me in Richard's barn some thirty-five miles away. Even though I had been driving the truck since I was seven, I was not prepared or licensed to operate a motor vehicle on public roads. What would I say to the officer while being arrested? It would be difficult enough to explain why I was driving the truck, much less explain that I was going to pick up my motorcycle. While watching Brando, I had seen how cops treated bikers. I didn't want to risk being beaten and thrown in prison. Even though I was fully capable of driving myself, I decided to ask Dad to taxi me to Wilton. After much nagging, he finally agreed and drove the Studebaker truck to pick up my new project, the Enfield. Little did I know it would be almost exactly three years and a national tragedy later before the Enfield would run again.

CHAPTER 8
OH, THE TIMES,
THEY ARE A-CHANGIN'

My Dad was a hard worker. Raising three kids, farming, milking cows, custom combining and baling hay, he seldom had time to rest. In the middle of all that, he decided to build the family a new house. He had worked very briefly for his uncle, George Brose, building homes in Bismarck. Somehow, he had scraped together enough money to buy a comprehensive book on modern carpentry. He read it every chance he got. So did I.

In 1956, Dad, Mom, and I traveled to Mountain Lake, Minnesota to see a featured home in *Farm Journal* magazine. It was magnificent! It had indoor plumbing and central heat topped off with an all-brick exterior. *Who were these people that could live in such a palace?*

Dad and Mom acquired the plans and presented them to the Farmers Home Administration (FmHA) to secure a loan. FmHA said it would cost twenty-five thousand dollars for the home they *wanted* to build and proclaimed we only qualified for a fourteen thousand dollar loan. After scaling back the plans, they reached a design compromise, and construction on our new home began in the fall of 1957. Soon, fall turned to winter.

I had strokes of luck, but so did my Dad. The winters in North Dakota do not typically lend themselves to outdoor projects, but this winter was different. It was one of the mildest winters on record. Dad hired a contractor with a backhoe to excavate the foundation and basement. He then built the concrete forms by hand. After pouring the footings, members of the surrounding families came to our farmstead and used shovels and wheelbarrows to mix and pour the basement walls. It was an outstanding community project. One more hurdle to go, and we would be home free.

By now, it was late November. Average nighttime temperatures were around fifteen degrees. Freezing temperatures could ruin the fresh concrete. I remember Mom coming into my room to say our nightly prayers. As we knelt next to the bed, she asked God to control the weather and to please, "keep the frost away." I don't think it got below forty degrees that night.

Luckily, we got the roof on by February 1958. One day, I returned home from school to see my Dad and uncles shingling. It was sixty degrees—*in February*! Mom must've had a direct line to God. She had clout. I've been a firm believer in God ever since.

For the next two years, Dad and the rest of the family worked on the house every chance we got. We all learned plumbing, wiring, heating systems, framing, drywalling, taping, painting, and more.

Our old house was a disaster. Built around 1910 by the original homesteaders, the Unruh family, it was a tiny, two-story shack with a dirt basement. The main floor had four rooms: a kitchen, dining, living, and bedroom. The upstairs had two full bedrooms and two small storage rooms. In the early 1950s, when the house got electricity through the Rural Electrification Act, Dad added a well to our property, indoor plumbing to the kitchen sink, and installed an electric water heater in the basement. Before that, all water was transported by hand from the livestock well in pails and heated on the cooking stove. Every once in a while air would get into the plumbing system, causing rusty, smelly water to shoot from the kitchen faucet. It was thick with iron and perfect for foundry use. We didn't have the convenience of an indoor toilet and used the outdoor "three-hole" unit when nature called.

The house was scorching hot in the summer and unbearably cold in the winter. An oil stove in the dining room was used to heat the main floor. It was "the place to be" in the winter if you wanted to stay warm. In contrast, the heating system for the upstairs bedrooms consisted of a small metal grate in the floor, where heat would supposedly rise from downstairs and heat the rooms. It appeared the designer was from an area with a warmer climate, like San Diego, and hadn't experienced a North Dakota winter.

Most winter days were not that bad with lows around ten or twenty degrees, but occasionally an

Alberta Clipper would blast down from Canada. When that happened, temperatures of thirty degrees below zero were not uncommon. If the wind and cold got unbearable, Mom would stuff rags into the cracks around the doors and windows to keep the inclement weather out.

My bedroom was in one of the upstairs storage rooms, tucked under the stairs to the attic. It was not the Presidential Suite. It didn't have lights or the San Diego-inspired "hole-in-the-floor" heating systems that were in my sisters' bedrooms. When I was about four years old, I showed up for breakfast looking blue as a Smurf. Mom saw my condition and went into a panic. She laid my clothes directly on the oil stove and heated them until they started smoking. She dressed me, and as the blood returned to my skin, she turned to Dad and demanded swift action be taken to correct the problem before her youngest child froze to death.

Dad commented on how much better off *we* were growing up than how *he* grew up. What he failed to mention was that when he was growing up, he slept in a bed with his siblings to stay warm. I was all alone in a miniature version of our butcher, Lindy Lien's, meat locker. Once again, Mom came to the rescue. She made a feather tick comforter. A feather tick was made by sewing two blankets together and stuffing them full of goose and duck down. It was soft and toasty warm. As the temperatures dropped, my sisters and I (dressed in flannel pajamas and wool socks), would climb under the feather tick blanket, prepared for our night of toasty hibernation. In the morning, we would wake up to a Winter Wonderland.

The moisture from our breath would condense overnight and freeze onto everything in the room. *Eat your heart out, San Diego!*

We moved into our new house in late 1959. Before the interior was complete, Dad ran out of money, and the project would take another twenty years to finish. We did, however, have heat in ALL THE ROOMS! My bedroom even had a closet *and* lights! I had moved up to the Presidential Suite.

CHAPTER 9
INTERLUDE

As the year drifted into 1961, I concentrated on school, farm chores, and figuring out how to make money to buy parts. I had made a list of the components required to rebuild the Enfield. I needed a new connecting rod, big end bearing, small end bearing, gasket set, gas lines, a piston and rings, a battery, and various nuts and bolts.

I sent the list to Nicholson Bros. for a quote. Several weeks later, a letter arrived from Canada. My hands shook as I opened the letter.

"Parts requested: SIXTY-EIGHT DOLLARS."

It was crushing. *How could I raise that kind of money?* Legal methods seemed out of reach. My mind wandered. Gangster movies were prevalent on television. I had seen *Little Caesar* with Edward G. Robinson. I envisioned myself robbing a bank, standing behind "Rico" holding a bag filled with money, as the G-Men crashed down the door.

"Save yourself, kid!" Rico yelled as a hail of machine gun bullets rained down.

As my mind refocused, I absentmindedly felt for bullet holes and realized I was not a mobster, not even for sixty-eight dollars.

My fourth-grade class had just read *Treasure Island*. Reinforcing the images of gold and silver coin mountains was Walt Disney's *Disneyland,* a television show that featured the Disney version of the Robert Louis Stevenson classic. Maybe I could find some buried pirate treasure! After mulling it over in my still-developing ten-year-old brain, I concluded that pirates probably did not travel fifteen hundred miles from the nearest ocean to bury looted treasure in our pasture. Even if they had, I wouldn't know where to look. "*Damn crafty, those pirates*," I thought to myself.

I'd watched a television movie that depicted bootleggers making moonshine and selling it for money. We had grain to ferment for the hooch, and there were plenty of old combine parts I could use to fabricate a still, but how to sell the moonshine? We lived in a very religious Mennonite community. No one drank soda, much less liquor. Converting a bunch of Bible-thumping teetotalers into raging alcoholics would be difficult, even with my suave Christmas-card-and-garden-seed sales training. In my mind, if I made some illegal sales and was being chased down by ATF agents, I could probably outrun them in my Dad's Studebaker truck, but getting any sales would be far-fetched.

Think, Dwight, think. There must be another way.

It was lambing season. We didn't raise sheep, but my uncle, Orville Deckert, had a whole farm full of them. Orville, who was twelve years younger than my Mom, and his wife, Maria, lived on a farm one-half mile north of ours. Maria was an immigrant whose family had survived the invasion of Ukraine by the Russian Army. In one of the most under-reported stories of the century, the Russian Army, under Stalin, murdered hundreds of thousands of people in Ukraine after the war. Maria's family, the Hiebert family, was lucky to be alive. Our church had sponsored the Heiberts and provided them with a little farm.

When I was about four or five years old, Orville and Maria asked me to be the ring bearer for their wedding. I was very timid, so I kept refusing. Males of ring-bearer age were rare in our community, so eventually, they had to ask my girl cousin, Lois, to be their ring bearer. I've always regretted not accepting their request.

Being our 4-H leader, I had learned a lot about all things farming from Orville. Orville heard my Enfield dilemma and suggested I raise a 4-H lamb to earn the re-building funds. He would sell me a lamb for five dollars, and I could sell it in the fall for twenty-five dollars. The day the little lamb rode home with us was a special day in my life. I had been allowed to pick any lamb out of the flock, and this lamb had come up and nuzzled my hand. I knew he was mine. I named him "Lamb Chop" after seeing Sheri Lewis's lamb puppet on television. Lamb Chop was tiny, maybe a little over a foot high. Mom helped rig a bottle with a rubber nipple for feeding him. Since we had dairy cows, fresh milk was always available for filling the bottle. For the first several weeks, feedings were every few hours. As he drank from the bottle, his tail would wag so vigorously that it shook his whole body.

Lamb Chop grew and became my constant companion. Not many animals are cuter than baby lambs and goats, and this ball of fluff was no exception. We had a small, unused pen in the barn where he slept at night. After feeding him in the morning, I would let him out of his pen, and he would follow me around the yard. If I neglected to give him my full attention, he would jump, kick and headbutt me in the back of my legs. If we were working in the farm shop, he would stay close by, munching on dandelions and other sheep delicacies.

It would be far too dangerous to let a small lamb out in the pasture with the cows. I couldn't be with him all of the time, and as he grew, he needed more space than his small pen. I moved him into the lean-to on the side of the barn. The lean-to was used for cattle during cold winter nights but went unused in the summer. The lean-to was much bigger than the barn pen and would give him room to run when he was not playing with me. With sliding doors on each end, he would be safe from predators. I would spread fresh oat straw around the dirt floor and stack a couple of bales of hay in the corner for him as a snack.

One morning, when Lamb Chop was about three months old, I approached the barn, sensing something wasn't quite right. The lean-to door was slightly open. I slid open the door and saw the heinous scene. Tufts of white wool floated through the air and dotted the floor. In a corner was Lamb Chop's mangled, lifeless body. It was devastating.

The neighbor dog had somehow gotten into the barn and done this evil thing. I had spent so much time investing all my emotions into this little lamb, and now he was dead.

Later that summer, the same neighbor dog would kill my pet rabbit. The actions of one evil animal should not damn a whole species, but I've distrusted dogs ever since. A ten-year-old boy trying to be a man has mixed feelings about crying and controlling their emotions. I sobbed uncontrollably after each event. I still tear up when I think about that little lamb and my soft furry bunny. I guess I've never been much of a man.

CHAPTER 10
BIG RED REVIVAL

One-by-one the months ticked by until it was fall, then winter. As my pets' deaths faded from memory, I again concentrated on making money so I could rebuild the Enfield. My allowance was now fifty cents a week. Garden seed sales were good. Christmas card pre-season sales were great, plus, I had added a line of medicinal salve to my growing sales empire. Things were looking up.

I was back to riding Shirley's French racing bike, as a mode of transportation and missed the brief excitement Big Red had brought into my life. Larry had bought Big Red and, through his ingenious tinkering, made it a much more usable motorbike.

Larry and I had the same access to Reverend Lowen's old, moldy *Popular Mechanics* magazines. While reading one of the flying-car articles, an ad for a Clinton, two-stroke Panther engine caught Larry's eye. If a 1/2-horsepower engine had worked, a 2.5-horsepower engine would be space-age stuff! With that, I'm sure Larry had dreams of running Big Red at the Bonneville Salt Flats International Speedway, thereby setting a new World Record for the "Fastest Bicycle Ever Sold At The Bismarck Trading Post." Somehow, he scraped together the eighty-nine dollars required to buy the engine. Larry invited me to witness the unveiling of his creation, Big Red 2.0. Since I practically lived at their farm, an invitation wasn't necessary. I was going to be there.

The Clinton engine had come with the coveted "centrifugal clutch" and was mounted in the space once occupied by the washing machine engine. No belt tensioner was required, allowing the operator to have both hands on the handlebars. This beast might get up to fifty miles per hour, and at those insane speeds, safety was paramount.

It was a tense moment. Larry applied the choke, pulled the recoil starter cord, and the engine burst to life with the distinct sounds made by all two-strokes.

"WAAW-DING-DING-DING, WAAW-DING-DING-DING."

As Larry worked the lawnmower throttle on the handlebars, clouds of smoke filled the Buller's shop. Two-stroke engines require a mixture of oil and gasoline to operate. When running, they emit lots of smoke and other unburnt gases. The Clinton was living up to the two-stroke persona. Larry slipped the v-belt onto the pulley, pulled on his fuzzy, yellow "Handy Andy" farm gloves, and hit the throttle. The clutch engaged as intended and he was off like a rocket. Big Red 2.0 had grown a new pair of cojones.

I was growing up part of the baby-boomer generation. As we reached our teenage years, transportation options beyond bicycles became an essential part of our experience. The introduction of cheap imports in the 1960s created an increased interest in motorcycles, and they began to proliferate.

My cousin, Gary Deckert, had a 200cc Triumph Tiger Cub. Ronny Wagner had a Harley-Davidson Hummer and then a Honda Super Cub 50. Roger Hertz had a Honda CB160. Marvin Wetzel had a Honda CT90 Trail. Darryl Heimbuck had a Whizzer and his older brother, Wilmer, a 305cc Honda Dream. Jim Lang, coming from a family of wealth, had a 305cc Honda CB Super Hawk. Brent Coleman had a Yamaguchi 50 Scrambler, and later, a Montgomery Ward's Riverside Moped. Gene Eide bested everyone with a Honda CB450. I, however, was walking or riding Shirley's bicycle, since my Enfield lay in pieces in the shop.

I was doing what I could to get the Enfield ready; using my Mom's sewing machine to reupholster the seat and washing greasy parts in pans of gasoline to prepare them for painting.

I had read the section on Enfield's in *Modern Motorcycle Mechanics* dozens of times and could quote whole paragraphs from memory. Etched into my mind were illustrations of how the timing gears went together, the oil pump assembly and other engine-build items. A ten-year-old brain has lots of unoccupied space. I was filling mine with engine illustrations, point-gap clearances, carburetor settings, and magazine articles about flying cars.

CHAPTER 11
POLITICS

In 1960, my father was helping the newly formed political party, the North Dakota Democratic-Nonpartisan League *(an oxymoron of gigantic proportions)*. The year was busy for him politically. William Guy was running for his first term as North Dakota Governor, and my Dad often met with him and his staff to plan political strategy. John F. Kennedy and Hubert Humphrey were running against each other in the Democratic Party presidential primaries. In February, Senator Kennedy campaigned in Bismarck. My parents and other dignitaries met with him in the basement of the Peacock Alley and were awestruck! They returned home with renewed vigor and hope for the future. Later that summer, my parents and I traveled east to Fargo, North Dakota, to attend Senator Humphrey's campaign rally. Dad had the opportunity to meet with him privately, and we all got to shake his hand.

The fifties had been tough times for farmers on the upper Great Plains. Grain and cattle prices were low. Cream sales from the dairy operation were our only source of steady income. Many times our farm's total weekly earning would be less than twelve dollars. With virtually no income, my parents struggled to make the FmHA loan payments on our new house.

The Wing Public School lunch program charged each student seventy-five cents *a week* for a hot, noon meal in the school cafeteria. The school superintendent, Hallie Sorenson, was in charge of collecting the lunch money from the students. Numerous times students, including myself, could not pay the seventy-five cents when Mr. Sorenson would come to collect. He'd say, "We'll start a tab, and you can pay it later."

Looking back, I think he would pay the tabs out of his pocket and reimburse himself when, and if, students could repay, relying on their honesty.

The late fifties were also years of drought. Crop yields were horrible. I remember in 1959, after making one round in the field, Dad parked the combine. Where there should have been fifty bushels of wheat in the hopper, there was a shovelful. Not only were the crops poor, but we would also have to borrow money to purchase feed for our livestock. All these unfortunate events, which were no fault of any political party, caused many people to consider voting for a change in leadership. Eisenhower had been in office for eight years, and the North Dakota State Government had suffered through years of non-growth. Dad just happened to be in the right place at the right time. Guy and Kennedy won their elections, by a nose.

One of my prized possessions is a photo of Senator John F. Kennedy walking up the steps of the World War Memorial Building in Bismarck, with my Dad's Studebaker car framed in the background. Little did I know that three years later, Kennedy's life and my Enfield story would intersect.

CHAPTER 12
SACRIFICE OF ABRAHAM

1961 flew by, and soon it was 1962. By March 1962, I had enough money to order the parts needed to begin rebuilding the Enfield and had spent time further researching their history.

Enfield had its start in Britain in the mid-1800's. Their first products were sewing needles. By the end of the century, Enfield had expanded to bicycles and bicycle parts. Enfield also was a major component manufacturer for the Lee-Enfield rifle (one of the most famous and widely-used military rifles of all time). In 1901, Enfield, now renamed Royal Enfield, expanded into the growing motorcycle market. As the brand steadily evolved, they introduced various models. The Bullet 500cc model I had was part of the 350cc and 500cc models designed following World War II that were meant to provide basic, economical transportation. Surprisingly, the Bullet is still produced in India, making it the world's longest-running production motorcycle!

Finally, the long-awaited day arrived. With my Dad's help, we ordered the parts, and another wait began. Unfortunately, FedEx didn't exist in 1962. Trains *slowly* transported most freight. Today, Amazon subscribers expect "same-day" delivery; we operated in the *same-month* mindset. The weeks went by until we *finally* got a phone call from the freight depot in Wing (also known as the grain elevator) letting us know that my goods had arrived. The former train depot closed years before, and afterward, the railroad contracted with the grain elevator to handle the local freight.

Grain elevators are the skyscrapers of the prairie. Averaging around ten stories tall, these structures are built to handle and store grain until sale. About every ten miles or so, they appeared next to the railroad. Small towns grew up around them. The ten-mile spacing helped farmers. A horse and wagon could only travel about twenty miles a day, so a farmer hauling grain would travel the ten miles to the nearest elevator, and then travel the ten miles home.

The city of Wing wasn't located on the main railroad line but on a branch line mostly used for collecting railroad freight cars filled with wheat. The branch rail lines were usually twenty miles from, and parallel to, the mainline to maintain the ten mile radius farmers needed to sell or buy grain.

The Wilton-Pingree Railroad, or WPRR, was our only link for freight until many years later when freight truck companies appeared. The WPRR did not haul enough cargo, other than wheat, to warrant an engine and freight cars, so they employed something called the "Goose" for hauling freight. Why it was called the "Goose," I'm not sure, but it could be described as a freight car with a diesel engine, making it self-propelled. Some people said it was called the "Goose" because its horn sounded like a goose. Other people said it was a "Goose" because it waddled back and forth as it went down the uneven tracks. Whatever the reason for its name or nickname, the "Goose" had delivered my parts to the Wing elevator.

Dad and I jumped in the truck and headed to Wing. As we drove up to the elevator, I could feel my heart pound in my chest. *Finally,* the project was moving forward. We strode into the elevator office. Dad plopped down into an old oak chair and lit a Lucky. He immediately struck up a light-hearted conversation about how dry it was, and when would it rain and …yadda, yadda, yadda… with the elevator manager. I was getting impatient. I had waited two years for this moment, and now we were talking about the weather?

My mind screamed, *"WHAT ARE YOU WAITING FOR? GET ON WITH IT!"*

Scanning the elevator office, I couldn't see anything that looked like my freight. Layers of grain dust covered every surface. Outlines of various depths remained where purchased items once sat. The place smelled of farm chemicals and cattle feed.

HAD I BEEN SCAMMED OUT OF MY SIXTY-EIGHT DOLLARS? WAS THIS A JOKE?

As Dad's conversation concluded with the long-range weather forecast, the topic of freight finally came up.

"Oh, yeah," said the manager, "it's in the warehouse."

The elevator held all rail freight in a separate, locked warehouse, so as not to co-mingle with their inventory. We walked to the warehouse, the manager opened the door, and THERE IT WAS! For me, it was as good as finding pirate treasure in the pasture! Boxes of smaller items were all packed into two bigger boxes. The manager asked us to check if everything was there and in good condition.

I opened the boxes and inspected the items one-by-one. Everything was fine. The manager reached down and picked up a large, red tag.

"Well, as soon as you take care of this, you can go," said the manager.

Dad asked, "What's the red tag for?"

"Customs Duty and freight charges," replied the manager.

"How much?" asked Dad.

"Looks like eight dollars for freight and eighteen for Customs Duty."

"*WHAT?!*" I thought.

In today's vernacular, I suppose I would have thought I was "being hassled by The Man," but it was 1962, and I wasn't yet introduced to "The Man."

"I didn't know anything about any of this!" I blurted.

The manager asked for the copy of the quote I had used for my checklist and studied it for a while.

"Right here," he pointed out, "it says, 'FOB Saskatoon, Saskatchewan, Canada.'"

At twelve years old, I was not exactly an import mogul, neither was my father. We had no idea what "FOB" meant.

"What does that mean?" I asked.

"Free On Board. It means that the freight charges to ship your package from Canada and the duty charges to get it across the United States border are in addition to whatever you paid for this stuff," he replied. "You can't have your goods until the bill is paid off."

My mind reeled, and visions of mobster movies again danced in my head, but this time I was wielding the machine gun. As my make-believe machine gun spit fire, I imagined neighbor dogs and customs agents writhing in agony.

When the anger subsided, I began crying. I was a twelve-year-old version of the Biblical character, Job. *What plight would God curse me with next?* I was expecting a plague of locusts to ascend, or the sky to begin raining frogs. Then, I remembered my Dad's weather conversation. Frogs were not in the forecast, at least not today.

After ordering parts, I only had about fifteen dollars left of my nest egg and still needed to buy paint and other items for the rebuild. I also wanted to buy some new fall clothes for school. I wasn't trying to make a fashion statement, but I had outgrown my rags from last year, and the "holes-in-the-tennis-shoes" look was not in vogue.

Dad opened his mouth and uttered the words, "I'll pay for it, and you can pay me back when you can."

I was dumbfounded. Dad NEVER had the money to pay for anything. When times were tough, he even rolled his cigarettes to save money. Using papers and Prince Albert Tobacco he could roll a cigarette one-handed, a skill even a child can appreciate.

As he looked me in the eye, he again said, "You can pay me back when you can."

Now I felt like a prodigal son reuniting with his father. Overcome by emotions, I had another cry, followed by hugging my Dad. He wrote a check, and we loaded the "stuff" into the truck. Now, I had two reasons to appreciate my Dad. He could roll cigarettes with one hand *AND* finance my motorcycle project.

He was very quiet on the way home. He never talked about the FOB charges again, but to pay for them, I think he sacrificed his smoking vice for a while, and probably missed some of the farm loan payments.

CHAPTER 13
SUPERSONIC

The late fifties had been a farming disaster but by 1962 farming was a spectacular success. Rains came early and often. Our cattle stood in the belly-deep grass all summer, and we harvested bumper crops. As the saying goes, "Make hay while the sun shines," and we did. Hay was everywhere! I would mow and rake it, and as soon as it was dry enough, Dad would bale it. The bales were loaded in the hay wagon, hauled home, and unloaded by hand into huge pyramids. The pyramids of bales were used to feed our cattle herd through the long winter.

1962 was also the year of the Cuban Missile Crisis. Since many of the Minuteman missile silos were in North Dakota, our state was a strategic target. Our farm was in the military flyway between the Grand Forks Air Force Base, and air bases in Rapid City, South Dakota, and Denver, Colorado.

Every hour or so, a Boeing B-52 Stratofortress bomber would lumber directly over our farm. Impossibly huge, the "B-52" bombers looked like large buildings suspended in the air. They flew so low it appeared as if they were following the contour of our hilly farm. As the Cuban crisis escalated, fighter jets would fly over in Delta formations at high speed. In 1962, it was still legal to fly supersonic over the continental United States, and sonic booms were a daily occurrence. Some booms were so loud and powerful, the house would shake, and the windows would rattle. It would be dead quiet and then, "BOOM!" The unexpected noise was scary.

SR-71 "Blackbird" military planes were being tested over North Dakota as well. Occasionally a jet would fly by so quickly, by the time we heard the sound of the engine, it had traveled from horizon to horizon. The high altitude, high-speed jets could fly faster than the speed of a .30-06 rifle bullet. The experience was terrifying and exciting at the same time.

After learning to hide under our school desks in case of an attack, the Cuban Missile Crisis resolved, and we resumed our normal lives sitting in the desks, rather than cowering under them.

Larry was becoming a certifiable, scientific maniac. He had read somewhere about "porting two-stroke motors," and with a simple hand file and sandpaper, he had ported the Clinton engine, now bolted to Big Red 2.0. Larry also had read about "expansion chamber exhaust systems" as a means of increasing horsepower. With basic tools, he had somehow fabricated an expansion chamber and fitted it to the engine exhaust. The transformation in sound and power was immense. I'm not sure what the top speed was, but the roar was amazing. I could hear Larry ride Big Red 3.0 all the way to Heimbuck's farm, some three miles away. I doubt if Isle of Man residents, listening to the motorcycles racing in the famous TT, had ever been treated to better mechanical noises. Now Big Red had cojones *and* horns.

Cousin Larry was a racer at heart and had laid out a one-mile track, most of it on other people's property. He would blast west down our driveway, turn north through our yard at full tilt, exit our yard through the tree rows on the way to Orville's, turn in Orville's yard heading east, and then back to his yard after turning south.

A two-stroke engine with an expansion chamber at full throttle sounds like a wailing Banshee. Larry managed to time his racing practice to coincide with our milking. As Larry rocketed through our yard at full bore, the dogs would give chase adding to the racket. The noise would cause the cows to kick, and the cats would run to find cover. Mom would look up from her milk pail and yell over the noise, "THAT CRAZY FOOL!"

Mom was very observant and more than half right.

CHAPTER 14
CHOICES

I managed to pay off the Duty charges loaned from Dad and had enough money leftover to buy paint. To me, colors are important. The Enfield had been painted black, but it seemed so common and blah. I wanted something extreme.

Over the years, I had requested marketing literature from Harley-Davidson. Even though my letters were handwritten and crude, they always were kind enough to send me their beautiful brochures featuring the latest offerings from "The Motor Company." The XLCH Sportster in *fuchsia* and the Duo-Glide in *turquoise* were terrific.

When building our new house, my parents had made a serious lapse in judgment. I was allowed to pick out any color I desired for my new room. After having spent my youth in a three-by-seven-foot space under the attic steps, with exposed plaster walls, somehow shades of tan and gray did not appeal to me.

After reviewing all of the Pittsburgh Paint paint swatches, I chose *fuchsia*. My parents assumed I was going blind and commented that fuchsia was not a proper color for a boy's room. I hunted down the XLCH brochure with the fuchsia motorcycle and pointed out that they were old-fashioned and needed to get up-to-speed on the latest design trends; I had become a veritable nine-year-old Frank Lloyd Wright. Eventually, we painted the bedroom fuchsia; it was so bright I seldom needed to turn on the lights.

I remember Uncle Art's first tour of our new home. He entered my room, squinting to shield his eyes from the brightness. He made an off-beat comment about being reminded of "bomb blasts" in World War II. I never quite understood what he meant; I loved the color.

Since I'd painted the Presidential Suite fuchsia, the Enfield would be turquoise. Occasional family trips to Bismarck to buy groceries and farm parts highlighted my dull life. These trips were my chances to catch up on big city life. Mom would sit down and make her grocery lists from the Wednesday edition of the Bismarck Tribune. The Tribune had the sales ads for all the grocery stores in Bismarck. She'd go through each ad and write down what store had the cheapest grocery item she needed. Bananas were five cents a pound at Brown's; flour was seventy-five cents a bag at Red Owl, and so on. Mom would spend ten dollars on gas for the car to save five dollars on groceries. If the store had a good comic book section for kids, I would stay and read about Uncle Scrooge McDuck's fabulous wealth, or Huey, Dewey, and Louie's adventures as Junior

Woodchucks. If Mom had a lot of shopping at one store, rather than wait, Dad went to a different store to do his shopping. If the grocery stores where Mom was shopping were not "child-friendly," I would accompany my Dad.

One of Dad's haunts was Hedahls, an auto parts store. It was an amazing place of everything automotive. My Uncle, Leo Bachmeier, worked at the store. Leo had also married one of Dad's intelligent sisters, Maxine. At a family get-together, Leo and I had had a conversation about paint (I was a dull child). During our discussion, Leo offered to mix the paint for my motorcycle and said that I should stop by the store when I was in town.

On this particular trip to Bismarck, Dad was going to Hedahls, so I tagged along, bringing my nest egg and paint swatches. While Dad shopped the aisles, Leo and I went to the paint section of the store. I showed him my turquoise swatch. I was downtrodden when he said the sample I liked was house paint, and he didn't sell house paint. Then, Leo boosted my spirits when he said he could match it with *automotive paint!*

Out came the *DuPont Automotive* paint catalog. We found a near-perfect color match. We calculated since I only had to paint two fenders, the front fork and a frame, a single quart would be adequate. Twenty minutes later, and five dollars less money in my nest egg, I walked out of the store with a quart of "Ford Caribbean Turquoise" tucked under my arm. I was fast becoming an enlightened gentleman. I now understood that there were two kinds of paint, house *AND* automotive.

CHAPTER 15
WORKING THE CANVAS

My life's paint and painting experiences have been long and dismal. It probably started with chewing the lead paint off my crib. My earliest recollection of painting, was when I was four years old.

In 1945, my older brother, Daryl, passed away from a kidney infection at the age of five. During the war, penicillin was available only for military use. A simple shot could have saved his life, but instead, my parents were forced to suffer through a year of agony watching him die (my mom was able to get the hospital bills paid off a mere thirty years later in the 1970's).

Every year, Mom would go through an annual ritual of showing me a box of Daryl's items. It held a little cowboy shirt, a Gene Autry cap gun, photographs, and a few simple toys. We both had tears in our eyes as she put the box of items away for another year. I had inherited two toys from Daryl: a pedal car and a coaster wagon. I enjoyed them both immensely. By 1954, the coaster wagon was faded and beginning to rust. It needed paint.

Luck smiled on me as Dad was painting the barn a bright red. I asked if I could use some paint for the wagon. He gave me a six-inch brush and a little paint in a gallon can, and sternly said, "Don't get any paint on yourself."

I parked the wagon on a little bit of grass in front of the barn and got busy. After painting all the top surfaces, I stood back, admiring my work. Soon, I realized the job wasn't complete until the underside of the wagon was painted as well (and this is where the brain damage from eating lead paint kicked in). Rather than tipping the wagon over to paint the bottom, I chose to crawl under the wagon with the six-inch brush. Every time the brush needed more paint, I crawled out, and then back under, to continue painting. *I was a genius!* What I didn't realize was that the brush was dripping bright red paint all over me, my clothes, my hair—*everything was covered in red paint!* Then, I remembered Dad's warning about not getting paint on myself.

Uh-oh, Dad is going to be very angry.

Trying to avoid the death penalty, I ran for the house and asked Mom to wash me. In 1954, barn paint consisted of linseed oil, white lead, turpentine, and other substances, some of which are now banned. It wasn't modern, non-toxic, latex paint that can be easily washed off with soap and water; this was sticky oil paint.

Mom tried homemade soap, Comet, Murphy's Oil Soap—*nothing worked!* The masses of oily red paint on my skin and hair were congealing into clumps.

Mom realized she needed to do something fast. She grabbed some rags, and we sprinted to the gasoline storage tank.

Farmers used gasoline engines in engine-powered equipment and stored the gasoline in large elevated barrels. When gas was needed to fill a tractor or truck tank, gravity would fill the hose and run into the equipment tank through a nozzle. Mom and I reached the gasoline tank, and she ran some gas into a pan. After soaking a rag in the gas, she said, "Close your eyes, Dwight."

She started scrubbing me vigorously from head to foot with gasoline. The gasoline dissolved most of the red paint, but it burned my skin and filled my lungs with fumes. I thought my scalp would catch on fire. It felt like she was pouring acid on my head. After a ten-minute gas wash, Mom said, "That's all we can get now, you need a bath."

At four years old, I was still small enough to fit in the kitchen sink. Mom ran some rusty hot water, put in some dish soap, and submerged me in the mixture. The soapy water felt soothing on my skin, but since the gasoline had softened most of the paint, it now dissipated and the white porcelain sink immediately formed a red scum line around its edges.

She furiously scrubbed until I was mostly clean—except for my hair. I had naturally thick, blond hair. Now, I had even thicker, RED hair. The color had set, and nothing short of paint remover would strip it. Luckily, we didn't have paint remover, or I probably would have been a human test subject.

Television programming was abundant with World War II movies. I had just watched one on our new

GE television. My imagination was activated. I envisioned myself in a prisoner-of-war camp. This secret camp was set up for the sole purpose of conducting paint-remover tests. I could hear the Nazi scientist saying, "Bring in ze next wictim, und restrain him."

I fought the guards as they tied me to a chair. One of them took out a container of a foul-smelling chemical.

"Now ve vill zee if the experimental paint remover vorks," said the guard.

I screamed as my face melted while he poured the concoction on my head. As my skin vaporized, exposing my skull, the Nazi Scientist, sensing success, cheered, "Look! Da paint ez disappearing."

A short time later, my hair was dry, and Mom gave her red-headed son the once over. My skin was clean, but my hair? Mom got out her sewing scissors and proceeded to cut red clumps from the tangled wad of dried paint on my head.

"That's the best I can do without cutting off all your hair," she said dejectedly.

As she held her makeup mirror to my face, I was startled by my appearance. My eyes were bright red from the gasoline, and my hair was a combination of red spikes and blond valleys. In some places, my scalp showed through the mess. I looked like a punk rocker. As I stared at myself in the mirror, I thought, *"Well, the wagon ended up great, I escaped the death penalty from Dad, AND my face was still intact (not melted off by some Nazi experiment)—with all this good fortune, a life of enchantment is sure to follow!"*

After the "wagon incident," I avoided painting whenever possible. However, the Enfield was waiting for its turquoise paint job. I was not aware of aerosol spray-paint cans in 1962, or that would have been my product of choice. I pulled out the quart of paint I had purchased at Hedahls. Now was the time to use it. After sanding the parts and the frame to a perfectly smooth surface, they were ready for paint.

Our shop was small but organized. Dad had rigged up an overhead track-of-sorts for moving engines and working on tractors. We worked to suspend the bike frame and other parts from the track with wire and prepared to spray them.

While suspending the parts, we noticed Mom enter the outhouse, which was visible directly east of the open garage door. Even though our new house had indoor plumbing, including a bathroom with a toilet, we used the outhouse whenever the weather was pleasant. The house used a septic system which was fickle at best and a plumber's nightmare at worst. We assumed the outhouse had no breakable parts—we were wrong.

Shortly after Mom entered the outhouse, Dad and I heard an earth-shattering scream. Looking up, we saw the outhouse door burst off its hinges, followed by Mom running to the house, her undergarments falling by the wayside. I'm sure we had just witnessed a new record for the hundred-yard dash. Dad and I went to inspect the toilet. Coiled up in the corner of the outhouse was a giant bullsnake. Mom had unknowingly entered the small, dark room and as she sat down to do her business, her eyes adjusted to the dim light. There in the corner, she saw the huge snake and had made her hasty exit. Apparently, the outhouse did have a part that could break, the door, but it was an easy fix. A few wood screws later it was repaired.

Dad and I returned to the shop and resumed preparations to paint the Enfield. Some years earlier, Dad had obtained a paint sprayer, which he had used to paint the outside of our new house. I knew nothing about painting with a sprayer, but from my wagon experience, I realized a paint brush would not create the glossy, smooth, automotive luster I desired. My goal was to duplicate the turquoise in the Harley-Davidson "Duo-Glide" brochure.

The whole sprayer unit consisted of a small, electric air compressor connected to a hose. The opposite end of the hose connected to the sprayer. The sprayer had a screw-on quart cup that held the paint, a pistol grip handle with a trigger, and a nozzle. The nozzle's function was to break the paint pigments into a fine mist.

"Do-It-Yourself" videos did not exist in 1962. Our paint-spraying education was non-existent. We had used the sprayer on the house, where it seemed to work just fine. We didn't realize automotive paint was thinner than house paint and each type of paint required a different nozzle; our nozzle was for house paint.

My excitement grew as I poured the contents of the Dupont paint can into the sprayer cup. I looked at Dad for encouragement.

He said, "It's your project, son," and handed me the sprayer.

I was too uneducated to try a test subject first. I went directly to the parts hanging from the wires and pulled the trigger. At first, a beautiful turquoise mist came from the nozzle, but within seconds it was producing sputters of paint, followed by shooting thin streams.

Without realizing it, I was ruining the paint job. I watched as the paint covered all the surfaces. When I finished spraying, I blew the turquoise snot from my nose and inspected the parts. The final finish was *HORRIBLE!* Every surface looked as if had been covered with dripping turquoise candle wax. It was the worst paint job ever!

This time there were no incantations. I swore. Dad gasped at the extent of my vocabulary. I think he was impressed. He thought he was raising a Navy man, maybe even an Admiral. I told my Dad, "I don't care anymore," and walked back to the house with tears in my eyes.

For now, I was done trying to be a painter.

The eternal optimist, Mom was always trying to cheer people up. That night at the supper table, after hearing the painting tragedy, Mom smirked, "At least you didn't get paint in your hair," referring to the "wagon incident" years earlier.

I was in no mood for humor.

I sarcastically replied, "Why don't you tell us about your toilet adventure?"

Mom's smirk turned to a frown. Dad grinned. We ate the rest of our meal in silence.

CHAPTER 16
A CHRISTMAS CAROL

Because of the favorable weather, 1962 was a busy year on the farm. As fall turned to winter, I realized the only tangible progress on the Enfield was the "candle-wax" paint job. The new parts still lay in boxes. The freeze came early, and it was much too cold to work in the shop after school.

Our little shop was about twenty feet wide and thirty-five-feet long. It had a small heating stove in which we burned used motor oil, but it took twenty-four hours for the shop to be sufficiently warm to enable human habitation. Checking my school schedule, I noticed this was one of those great years when students would have two full weeks of uninterrupted holiday vacation to celebrate Christmas and the new year.

I sat down with Dad and had a heart-to-heart conversation. I had worked very hard for him that year. He owed me something for all my labors.

"Would you help me work on the Enfield during the school break?" I asked.

He looked me in the eye and said, "Sure Dwight, we'll work on it together."

I was euphoric.

Two weeks off working with my Dad? It would be a wonderful vacation!

The weeks flew by, and soon it was the week before Christmas. The winter weather had warmed enough to work in the shop, and I busied myself getting everything organized for the upcoming two weeks. Since the new engine parts from Nicholson Brothers were coated with Cosmoline to prevent rusting, I cleaned them and prepared them for installation.

On an evening in mid-December, a car pulled into our driveway. It was my uncle, Henry "Hank" Deckert, and his son, Dennis. Hank, and his wife, Doris Jean, lived on a farm one mile south of ours. Dad and Hank were the same age and good friends. Mom welcomed them into our house, hugged her brother, and escorted them to the living room where Dad and I were watching *McHale's Navy*. Dad and Hank exchanged pleasantries before Hank dropped the bombshell.

"Say," he began, "I need to overhaul the engine in my Ford truck, and Dennis and I were wondering if we could use your shop over the holidays. You've got that overhead track we can use to pull the engine."

I was sure my Dad would inform Hank that OUR shop was busy those two weeks to work on the Enfield. What came out of his mouth was, "Sure thing, Hank. I'll start the stove on Friday night. You can come by Saturday morning, and we'll get started."

Now, the little shop would be filled with Hank's Ford truck parts, impeding our progress on the Enfield. There wasn't adequate room for both projects. Hank and Dennis could have picked *any time* to use my Dad's shop, why these particular weeks? Dad could have scheduled them for another time. To me, Dad's answer to Hank was unfathomable.

Once again, I was devastated. I was frustrated and furious. Did my Dad's solemn oath to his son mean nothing? My father had lost my trust and respect. Never again did I have faith in any promise he made to me, and I vowed to leave the farm the moment I graduated high school.

The two precious weeks of the 1962 Christmas vacation holiday passed with no further progress on the Enfield. The project would have to wait until the next summer.

CHAPTER 17
THE CASE OF THE MISSING CASE

The weather of 1962 carried into 1963. It rained frequently and, between the rains, we worked frantically to plant crops and make hay. In late July, a three-day monsoon restricted us to the indoors. I asked Dad if we could work on the Enfield until things dried out. He reluctantly agreed, and we began moving the parts from the back of the shop to the work area.

I had overlooked the broken crankcase. Years before, when Uncle Richard broke the connecting rod the second time, the broken rod had removed a chunk of aluminum from the crankcase flywheel housing. The housing needed repair, and the fix was *WAY* beyond my mechanical capabilities.

The Enfield crankcase had two halves. Split vertically; it had a left and a right side. Bearing bores (holes) were in each half to support the horizontal crankshaft. Inside each crankcase housing was cast an integral, individual housing to separate the flywheel from the crankcase oil. The impact of the rod broke one side of the internal flywheel housing. It needed repair, but how?

Dad may have had some faults, but being mechanically dull was not one of them. With just basic tools, he could repair almost anything. He even successfully disassembled and rebuilt the automatic transmission in our Studebaker car.

Dad analyzed the broken flywheel housing and formulated a plan of repair. He first drilled holes into the edges of the broken housing. He then removed flux from several welding rods and inserted them into the drilled holes. The web of welding rod wire formed a miniature rebar system, like that used to strengthen concrete. From sheet metal, he then formed an inner and outer mold and clamped it to the housing. Next, he grabbed an old aluminum piston from the junk pile outside the shop. Using a hammer, he broke the piston into small pieces and placed them in a crucible. Years before, when we built our house, Dad had purchased the crucible. Prior to plastic plumbing, sewer pipes were made of cast iron. The cast iron joints were sealed by filling them with oakum and molten lead. Fortunately, he still had the crucible. It was essential to repairing the Enfield.

Now, Dad needed to melt the aluminum pieces in the crucible. We didn't own an acetylene torch, and a propane torch doesn't generate enough heat to melt aluminum. The answer was in the corner of our shop —the electric welder. The Forney farm welder had come with a carbon arc attachment. It had two carbon rods. Bringing the rods together caused a hot electric arc to flash between them. The electric arc attachment was so dangerous it required wearing a welding helmet with eye-shielding, green-glass inserts and proper gear.

"Z-Z-H-M-M-M-M."

The sound of a strong electric arc filled the air. A light brighter than the sun illuminated the shop. You could see why early movie projectors used carbon arc lamps for their source of illumination. As he applied the arc to the aluminum, molten metal filled the crucible.

"STAND BACK!" he shouted, as he laid down the carbon arc torch and picked up the crucible. The alchemist then carefully carried the crucible to the crankcase and began pouring the molten, silver-colored, aluminum metal into the mold. The thin metal used to make the mold was zinc plated, and as the hot, molten, metal burned off the plating, the sweet smell of toxic zinc oxide fumes filled the air. *"Hopefully these fumes are an antidote to the lead paint I ingested as a child,"* I thought.

"It'll take a while for it to cool and solidify. We'll check it after milking the cows," Dad explained as we walked to the barn.

"Hate" is a word I don't use lightly, but I *HATED* milking and *HATED* milk cows. I felt that when God created Holsteins, he must have gone fishing and left Lucifer in charge. They were the stubbornest, meanest animals on the farm and, although they were stubborn, and mean, they were not stupid. A herd could find a gate left open six miles away, and they could be there in five minutes. *Were they being teleported?*

I was reminded of their cow-teleportation capabilities years later while watching the transporter sequences on *Star Trek*. Scenes from an imagined episode, "The Wrath of Bessy," now flashed before me. I could see the bridge from the Enterprise with a herd of Holsteins in the transporter, ready for teleportation.

"We have enough milk for now Scotty. Beam them back to earth," says Captain Kirk.

"Ey-Ey, Captain. These cows made a real sloppy mess of things. The floors will never be clean again," replies Scotty.

The transporter was powered up.

"B-R-R-N-N-G."

The cows were magically gone. A gang of Klingon slaves cleaned up the manure and straw, while the cows, returned to earth, were shown running to an open gate and escaping to their freedom.

Twice a day, every day, the cows needed milking. It was like a life sentence without the possibility of parole. We always arrived late to family get-togethers and had to leave early, so that we could milk the cows. Not only was milking mentally and physically taxing, but we milked our twenty cows BY HAND! All our enlightened neighbors (and even the non-enlightened ones) used milking machines to milk their cows, but not my parents. We had a milking machine, but it had been relegated to serve as a barn adornment, rather than a working milking machine. Dad had purchased it used at a farm auction and proudly installed it in our milking parlor. In reality, Mom was in charge of most business decisions, and when the cows gave slightly less milk with the milking machine, she banned it from ever being used again. "Why use a milking machine when we have child labor?" she must have thought. My thoughts involved ground beef, or to be more precise, ground Holstein.

After evening milking, I ran to check the outcome of the Enfield casting. The parts had cooled, and I removed the clamps holding the forms in place. It was a beautiful sight. A new, perfectly-formed, crankcase housing wall now existed. However, the top edge of the new casting would need machining to mate with the unbroken housing. *How could sophisticated machining be accomplished with hand tools?* I would need Dad to work some more alchemy, and he did.

The next day it was pouring rain as we resumed work on the engine case. The original top edge of the flywheel housing had a notch around its entire circumference. This notch mated with a groove in the opposite flywheel housing. Somehow, we needed to machine the notch into the newly-casted wall of the housing. Thankfully, aluminum is a material easily machined with a hardened piece of steel.

Working his alchemy, Dad fitted a steel post to the crankshaft bore on the housing to act as a center-anchoring point. He then found a bearing that slipped over the shaft and attached a radius rod to the bearing. An old typewriter from the junk pile provided a hardened steel part that was ground to a chisel point and then clamped to the radius rod. As he dragged the sharpened tip around the center post, an elegant aluminum chip curled from its cutting edge.

After a few passes and some cutter adjustments, the machining was complete! Working as a machinist many years later, I would learn that Dad had fabricated a conventional device used in machining— a *trepanning tool*. Without formal training, I wasn't sure how he'd dreamt up the idea, but it was exactly what we needed at the time.

Now, finally, assembly of the Enfield could begin.

CHAPTER 18
SUCCESS AND TRAGEDY

Assembling the Enfield was left to me. I spent every free moment rebuilding the engine. The crankshaft was a bolted assembly. I disassembled it and installed the new big-end bearing and connecting rod and bolted the crankshaft back together. After installing new bearings and seals in the refurbished crankshaft housing, I applied a generous layer of shellac and slid the crankcase housing into place. The two housings fit together like a glove. I installed the bolts and tightened them. As the assembly progressed, the engine began to take shape. Somewhere between assembling the crankshaft, and bolting on the heads, I learned first-hand the mystery that is "British Engineering."

British Engineering is world-renowned. Names like McLaren Automotive, Lotus Cars, Merlin, Rolls-Royce, Spitfire, and others are synonymous with innovative, brilliant engineering. Then, there are some of the other British Engineering accomplishments. I assume the years after World War

II were difficult for them to overcome. Manufacturers were suffering. They had limited capital, bombs destroyed their facilities, entire workforces of people perished serving in active duty, and they were ruled under a Socialist government, causing tremendous burden.

Under this scourge, some of the emerging engineering logic was difficult to understand. It seemed as if the greatest minds in Britain had gotten together to conceive a great invention and at the last moment the local insane asylum had been put in charge to finish the design. Take American versus British bolts for example. When working on my Dad's tractor with American nuts and bolts, if I had a nut or a bolt that measured 3/4-inch across the top, I would use a wrench labeled "3/4" to tighten or loosen the bolt—simple. In contrast, the Royal Enfield used something called "British Standard Whitworth" fasteners. *What gems these were!*

Prior to the eighteenth century, each metal worker or blacksmith created bolts with unique diameters, thread pitches and head sizes. Begun in the 1800s, "Whitworth fasteners" were the first failed attempt to world-standardize threads, nuts, and bolts. The good folks at the British asylum, rather than label an open-ended wrench "3/4" to fit a 3/4-inch nut, decided to label wrenches using the diameter of the bolt *shank* (instead of the diameter of the nut, or the head of the bolt). So, if you had a 3/8-inch diameter bolt shank, the head of the bolt or the nut (the part you put the wrench on) would technically be .71-inches wide, and the wrench would be labeled "3/8". Next, the good folks at the asylum thought they could save metal by making nuts and the heads of bolts slightly smaller, and they reduced the size. So now, nuts and bolts with heads sized 7/16-inch could also use the .710 wrenches used on the 3/8-inch-shanked bolts. As a consequence, wrenches labeled "3/8" or "7/16" might fit on a bolt with a 3/8-inch shank or a 7/16-inch nut or bolt head—*or they may not fit at all! Brilliant British Engineering at its best! CUCKOO!*

What happened next was legendary. The British then changed all the thread pitches on the bolts to conform with metric standards but left the bolt diameter measurements in inches. Now, the 3/8-inch nuts would not fit on 3/8-inch bolts. The trouble continued late in the war when the British converted bolt diameters to metric sizes. I guess after causing all the confusion, why stop messing with a good thing? So, what had begun as a method of standardizing had created the most un-standardized system of nuts, bolts, and threads in history. Bolt size did not correlate to nut sizes; diameters were metric, not Imperial; items had Imperial labels, but, in fact, they were now metric and, to top it all off, there was no discernible relationship between the nuts and bolts and the sizes listed on the wrenches. The Quadfecta was complete! I'm sure it helped the English win World War II. Maybe the "The Whitworth Code" was all some devious plan by the British War Department to fool the Germans. The secret German Enigma code machines were designed to encrypt and decrypt the Enigma-coded messages sent by the Nazis. The British had a huge operation of mathematicians and scientists at Bletchley Park dedicated to breaking the code. It was unbreakable until eccentric, Alan Touring, invented the electronic computer and the Allies could read the Nazis' messages. While Hitler's scientists and generals were consumed trying to unravel "The Whitworth 'what-in-the hell-was-going-on-with-British-bolt-making' Code" the residents of the asylum won the war, and so did the Allies.

Uncle Richard had warned me about the "Whitworth bolt and wrench issues," and had included a set of Whitworth wrenches with the purchase of the Enfield. He should have included bandages and disinfectant. My Navy, verbal pre-training was coming along nicely as I sorted through piles of wrenches. None of them fit any nut or bolt on the Enfield. After bashing my knuckles to a bloody pulp from trying to tighten the British fasteners, I assumed I'd solved the origins of the British term "bloody."

Another example of the British Engineering & Asylum partnership at the time was Lucas Industries. In my experience, they proved to have smart-looking electrical gear and instruments that miraculously worked when least expected and failed miserably when most needed. It was apparent the residents in the asylum had more influence than just bolt-making.

School studies and farm chores consumed my time. Rebuilding the Enfield was temporarily put on hold. I would have to wait until next spring to finish the build; besides, it would be too cold to ride in the winter.

In the fall of 1963, as I started eighth grade, the country was alive with optimism. President Kennedy had launched several tax incentives that seemed to be working. The economy was picking up, and farm prices had risen. Russian missiles were no longer threatening the United States from Cuba. NASA was well on their way to putting a man on the moon. New cars and trucks appeared on the streets. The country was whole again. Then, tragedy struck.

It was a lovely late-November day. While sitting in Mr. McDonough's class, Superintendent Sorenson walked in the door.

"I have an announcement to make. President Kennedy was shot and killed in Dallas. The school buses will leave in fifteen minutes. School is postponed until further notice."

After hearing the news, Mr. McDonough clasped his head in his hands and said, "Oh no. God, no."

As we rode the school bus home, groups of three or four students huddled together discussing in hushed tones what had happened. Some of the older girls were crying. The forty-five-minute bus ride seemed to take hours.

The bus pulled into our driveway, I got out and went into the house. Dad was watching the events unfold on the television. I had never seen my Dad cry before. He was sobbing uncontrollably. I sat next to him, and he put his arm around my shoulders. Nothing was said as we watched Walter Cronkite and Dan Rather describe what had happened in Dallas. The world had changed.

CHAPTER 19
HOUSTON, WE HAVE IGNITION

The week of Thanksgiving 1963 Mom was visiting relatives in Canada, so Dad and I were alone. Before she left, she cooked us a ham and baked at least a dozen pies for us to eat during her absence. For supper, Dad fried potatoes and onions and served them with thick slices of the ham. Dessert would be a slice of Mom's outstanding pie. *Yum!* In between eating, milking, and watching the Kennedy funeral proceedings on television, Dad and I finished assembling the Enfield. The last to-dos were connecting wires, hooking up the battery, and final adjustments to the clutch and brake cables.

I remember that day like it was yesterday. Tuesday, the twenty-sixth day of November, nineteen sixty-three, in the year of our Lord. The weather was perfect. There were blue skies, it was sixty degrees, and the wind was calm. I rolled the Enfield to the middle of the farmyard, raised it on its rear stand, and filled its gas tank with gasoline. It was time to ride!

The procedure had gone through my head many times:

(1) open the fuel petcocks located under the colossal chrome gas tank,

(2) tickle the Amal carburetor until gasoline runs all over the new paint,

(3) apply the choke,

(4) retard the manual spark advance to prevent a broken leg,

(5) work the kick-starter until the engine is coming up on compression, and

(6) with all of my one-hundred pounds of strength, straighten my right leg while jumping on the kick-starter.

The mighty single-cylinder ticked over and—

Nothing.

Repeat.

Nothing.

Repeat.

With a cough, it burst to life! I busied myself working the choke, the throttle, and the manual spark advance as the engine warmed up. It had a deep bass sound. As I worked the twist-grip throttle, the handlebars shook. Frankly, I was intimidated. This bike was not Big Red. It was a *REAL* motorcycle with forty times the horsepower of the Briggs and Stratton. Growing up on a farm and attending rodeos, I felt like I was about to ride a bucking bull. I swung my leg over the saddle and pushed the Enfield off its rear stand. I pulled in the hand clutch, kicked the foot-shift lever into first gear, smiled at my Dad, goosed the engine, and let out the clutch- *I was off!*

Big-displacement, single-cylinder engines have vast reserves of torque. The Royal Enfield was no exception. As I gave it more throttle, it pulled like a tractor. When I shifted into second gear, the motorcycle lunged forward. Tapping the brake, I slowed for the turn. Exiting the turn, I kicked it into third gear and accelerated towards Larry's farm. With a real clutch, brakes, lights, and 30-horsepower, it was exhilarating!

I pulled into Larry's farm and parked in front of their shop. Larry came out and marveled with me at this bit of British engineering. I was beaming. Larry was envious. He jumped on Big Red 3.0, pulled the recoil starter and we went riding. Now we weren't just "bikers," we were a bad-ass gang. We would have gone to Wing or Tuttle and terrorized the townsfolk, but I had to get back home for milking. I also had to learn two new Bible verses for church Youth League the next night. The terrorizing and looting would have to wait for another time.

CHAPTER 20
SLOT CARS

We went riding all winter; Marvin Wetzel on his Honda Trail 90, Larry on Big Red 3.0, Darryl Heimbuck on his Whizzer, and me, on the Royal Enfield Bullet. We would ride from farm to farm, waving at neighbors as we roared through their yards, out-accelerating their farm dogs. We honed our riding skills driving on snow, ice, and mud. To quote the British, "We had a bloody good time."

On days or nights when it was too cold to ride, we needed something else to occupy our time. Slot car racing was all the rage. Uncle Orville and Aunt Maria's son, Jeffery (my cousin), was about four years my junior. He had received an Eldon slot car racing set for Christmas. During a family visit, we had a blast playing with it. It had fancy little cars with electric motors zooming around a track and hand controllers to adjust their speed. I made time to play with Jeffery and his race car set whenever I could. I was hooked.

At some point, I acquired a Strombecker slot car racing set of my own. After a while the small, figure-eight track became boring. Wild Cousin Larry came up with a solution. We would build ourselves a one-of-a-kind track! Mom's older brother, George, had an available table tennis top. It measured five feet by nine feet and was three-quarters of an inch thick. It was the ultimate platform for a slot car track.

We wanted a fast track, so I took pencil to paper and came up with a design that had maximum straightaways and corners with the largest radii that would fit on the sheet. Two big ovals that intersected at one end appeared to have the right features. Rather than the typical over-under bridge, our track would allow cars to crash at the intersection if the drivers did not control their speed. Larry approved the design, and we started building.

Some leftover two by fours worked well to make the table legs. We secured the table tennis top to the legs, creating a base. Then, we carefully drew the exact location of where to cut the slots. Using a long piece of angle iron as a guide and an electric hand saw, we perfected the straight slots, but how would we fashion the corners? Uncle George offered us the use of his router, but we had no bits of the correct size. Then I remembered the trepanning tool dad used on the Enfield crankcase. Larry and I retrieved it from the shop. Again, the tool worked splendidly, and we had perfect corners to match the straightaways. We purchased a roll of quarter-inch wide, self-adhesive, aluminum tape to use as the conductor for the slot cars. After delicately applying the aluminum tape to the track, we pounded small nails through the aluminum tape and out the bottom of the table, giving us a hidden location to make the wire connections. Larry designed and built precision guard rails made from brass welding rods bent to fit the corners. They were stunning! We were ready to race!

We hooked up the transformer from the Strombecker race set and hit the rheostats. Not much happened. This bigger track had more electrical resistance than the smaller figure-eight track and didn't have sufficient power. Once again, Larry came up with the solution. Some old car batteries had the right voltage to replace the transformer. They worked great! We were racing!

I spent many hours racing slot cars with family and friends. Learning about rheostat controls, brush motors, revolutions per minute, gear ratios, tire compounds, serial and parallel electric connections, and other related topics were now part of my education. Company names like COX, Revell, Pittman, Mitsubishi, Monogram, K & B, and Aurora filled the cavity between my ears. While studying in college, only a few years later, the lessons learned would contribute to my understanding of physics and engineering, leading to my future success. GOOD STUFF!

A friend of mine, Roger Hertz, lived twenty miles from our farm. He was a slot car enthusiast and showed up at the farm on his CB160. It was a *really* nice bike. We raced slot cars the whole afternoon, and as the sun began to set, he reached for his motorcycle helmet and jacket. I scoffed.

"It's much safer to drive with a helmet than without one," he said.

"I never really thought of it that way," I replied.

"I'm getting a new one. I'll sell you this one for five dollars," Roger offered.

It was a deal. We shook hands. From then on, my "bitchin' biker" image would include a helmet.

When traveling to Bismarck, a favorite haunt of mine was Sioux Sporting Goods. They had a massive inventory of camping supplies, sportswear, basketballs, model airplane parts (another hobby I enjoyed), guns and ammo, as well as an impressive selection of top-quality slot cars and components. Every red-blooded, pimple-faced geek within a one-hundred-mile radius of Bismarck made pilgrimages to the store whenever the opportunity presented itself. I loved the place; I fit right in.

In the early sixties, the store opened its "Honda Motorcycle Shop." Tucked away in the back were models of every description, size, model and color. Benlys, Super Hawks, Dreams, Super Cubs, Trail Models, Scramblers, and Super Sports lined the walls. This was my first exposure to modern motorcycles.

American and British motorcycles could trace their lineage to before World War II. These Japanese motorcycles were fresh designs that used modern engineering and manufacturing techniques. The floor was spotless; there wasn't a drop of leaking engine oil in sight. You could get electric starters, rear suspension, and amazing mileage all at a very affordable price—*the Super Cub 50 was rated at two hundred miles per gallon!* As I picked up some brochures, I noted the absence of Whitworth fasteners. From what I could tell, Japan's asylums didn't have field days.

The Honda brochures were enlightening with their full-color pages and lists of technical specifications. Marketing dream-building, they looked almost as good as the motorcycles. I memorized them all. A new vision was festering in my brain. *I was going to own a new Honda 305 Scrambler.* Now, I needed a strategy. I reasoned since the Enfield was running, it must be worth something as a trade-in for a new Honda. All I needed was enough money to pay the difference between the trade-in value and the price of the new Honda. Time to get to work and raise some cash.

I had another sit down with Dad. We decided that if I did all the land farming, Dad and Mom would agree to do all the cattle ranching and milking. When fall came, they then would pay the difference, and buy me a new Honda motorcycle. By not having to do farming, Dad would have time to do custom haying for neighbors, raising some extra cash. We had a deal!

CHAPTER 21
I WAS IN CHARGE

I had been doing much of the farming for several years. Now at the advanced age of fourteen, I was in charge. The International Harvester W-9 gas tractor strained to pull the three-bottom plow with the pony drill and packer; it was so ancient it wasn't even equipped with hydraulics.

At the time, tractor cabs were nonexistent. The plow and the pony drill had wheel-driven mechanisms to engage them. Whenever the operator pulled a rope, the mechanism would raise or lower the plow. The depth of the plow was set by reaching behind the tractor seat and adjusting levers that jutted out from the plow. The only semi-modern device was the trip hitch.

Our farm consisted mostly of rocks, mixed in with a little soil. If one of the plowshares hooked a rock, rather than break the plow, the hitch would trip, disengaging the plow from the tractor. The operator would then have to reverse the tractor and re-engage the hitch. However, the plow needed to get unhooked from the rock before moving forward. Being brilliant, we carried an industrial jack on the tractor, so we could jack up the plow to get over the offending rocks. The use of the jack required dismounting the tractor, getting the jack under the plow, jacking up the plow, slowly driving forward while the jack tipped over, dismounting the tractor, retrieving the jack, remounting the tractor and then continuing to plow. At the next rock, usually ten feet away, the process would repeat. This method was slow, mind-numbing work.

With all the rocks in our fields, I was spending more time jacking and backing, than I did plowing and seeding. The planting process was taking way too long. Something had to be done to speed it up. I measured the plow's mechanical, wheel-driven lifting device. It was longer when extended than when collapsed. *Why not replace it with a hydraulic system of the same dimensions?* Hydraulics would allow the plow operator to easily raise or lower the plow, enabling them to avoid the rocks, even while the wheels were turning.

A trip to Bismarck was warranted. As the name suggests, The Farm and Ranch Store on East Main Avenue had all things related to farming and ranching. Browsing through the selection of hydraulic cylinders, I found one appropriately sized. I also found a clever kit that contained an oil reservoir, hydraulic hoses, a hydraulic pump that mounted to the tractor power take-off, and a valve that was mounted near the tractor operator to control the flow of the hydraulic oil. To update the W-9, we *needed* this kit. I spent the entire spring parts budget to make the purchase but knew it would be worth it. For the rest of the season, I'd have to be extremely careful not to break anything.

Several hours later, mounting the hydraulic system was complete. The cylinder was attached to the plow, the hoses were connected, and I fired up the tractor. I engaged the power takeoff and moved the hydraulic valve lever. The plow went up and down. The hydraulic lift worked perfectly! Even people at the asylum have good days, and this was mine.

I attacked the spring planting with renewed vigor. The hydraulic retrofit was speeding things up and making a big difference. Instead of taking a month, I would be done planting in a week. What would I do with all the extra time? I decided to prepare more ground for farming.

Our farm was one section of land equalling six-hundred-forty acres. We farmed one-hundred-twenty acres, and two hundred acres consisted of pasture. Why wasn't half the farmland being used? Being situated on the edge of a glacial moraine, it was all rocks! As ancient glaciers marched forward, they pushed piles of rocks and dropped debris throughout the area. From what I could tell, our farm contained the majority of the discarded rocks. They ranged in size and shape from pebbles to small cars and were everywhere! No wonder our farmland was cheap- no one else must've wanted it! Now, it all made sense.

The early homesteaders plowed around the big rocks, making the fields a patchwork of small oddly-shaped strips ranging in size from three acres to forty acres. It was a mess! After I finished planting, I decided to start picking rocks to clear the ground to make more tillable acres. We didn't have a loader for our tractor, so everything was done by hand. We had a stone-boat, which is a flat sheet of heavy-gauge steel, connected to a chain and hooked to the tractor hitch. As I worked, I threw rocks that were small enough for me to wrestle by hand onto the stone-boat. Slightly larger rocks were levered onto the stone-boat using a crowbar. After collecting the rocks on the stone-boat and pulling it to a nearby rock pile, the rocks were unloaded by hand and stacked in huge piles. Some bigger rocks required digging around the base with a spade, attaching a log chain, and dragging them to the rock pile with a tractor. The boulders that were too big and cumbersome to be moved remained in place.

With all the physical labor, I had developed the strength of an ox. I was able to manually pick up rocks over two hundred pounds and place them on the stone-boat. However, one rock stumped me. My cousins from Bismarck, Bradley and Greg Hinkel, were staying with us for the summer. They were supposed to help me haul bales and pick rocks (but we all knew they came for my Mom's cooking). We came upon a grey-black colored rock slightly larger than a football. I could barely lift it! Bradley, who was also strong, could not lift it. It felt like it was more than three hundred pounds!

Meteorites had passed over Saskatchewan and North Dakota in ancient times. I now believe it was an iron-nickel meteorite, quite valuable today. Unfortunately, in the 1970s Dad buried our rock piles. I estimate it's under eight feet of soil. Treasure hunting with modern metal-detecting devices might be part of my future adventures!

CHAPTER 22
THE LEARNING CURVE

The rains continued in 1964 and crops were good. Dad was busy making additional income haying for neighbors while Mom and I did the farm chores. The rock picking continued until I had created a new, perfectly-square, forty-acre field. Dad was impressed and gave me one of the three compliments I received from him in my lifetime. The other two would occur when I married my beautiful wife, Sheila, and when I built our new house.

Internal combustion engines are marvelous things. How they work at all defies logic, illustrating the influence of those British asylums. To take a minuscule amount of fuel, introduce it to a combustion chamber and ignite it with a spark plug (with just the right amount of air to push down the piston and rotate the crankshaft) is insane. The vast amount of physics, chemistry, and engineering knowledge to support making an engine not only operate but operate reliably is mind-blowing. To consider that for more than a century continuous improvements have been made to this basic design is also awe-inspiring (but I'm getting ahead of myself).

The Enfield engine required human intervention to work correctly. The optimum time for the spark plug to fire varies with the speed of the engine. At slow speeds, the spark plug should fire slightly after the piston goes past the top or *After Top Dead Center*. As the engine speeds up, however, the spark plug needs to fire slightly *Before Top Dead Center*. This variance occurs because at higher speeds the pistons move up and down so fast that the flame in the combustion chamber needs to be lit earlier in the firing cycle, to maintain optimum pressure in the combustion chamber. Modern engines use automatic spark advance systems to perform this magic without the operator being cognizant of what was happening. Old cars used a manual spark advance system to run properly. While crank-starting a Model-T, my mother almost lost her arm when the engine backfired, blasting her forearm over the sharp edge of the license plate.

The Enfield's manual spark advance system operated with a lever on the handlebars. The operator, me, had to remember when starting the engine to retard the ignition to prevent the engine from firing too soon, causing it to backfire and violently lift the kick-starter.

Occasionally, the lead paint I had eaten as a child affected my memory and I would forget to retard the ignition after my last ride and before trying to kick-start the engine for the next one. I vividly remember two of these occasions.

To kick start the Enfield, I needed to park the rear stand on something firm. We had a small slab of concrete in front of our house that was the roof of the well-house, and it was just the right size. It was nice and solid so when I jumped on the kick-starter, the support stand had ample footing and the bike would remain upright, rather than sinking into the soft soil and tipping over. I went through all of the usual pre-start routines, but on this occasion, I had forgotten to retard the spark advance. I weighed about a hundred pounds at the time and needed every pound to kick over the 500cc single-cylinder engine. I would work the kick-starter until the engine was on the compression stroke and then leap into the air. At the top of the jump, I would lock my right knee and release all of my hundred pounds of fury into my right foot, which was on the kick-starter. On this occasion, as my energy was released and the kick-starter was about three-quarters of the way through its travel, the engine backfired. Now, instead of me pushing down, the engine and kick-starter violently raised me upward, about six feet into the air. I crashed into the house and fell between the foundation and the motorcycle. I can't explain how I wasn't injured, but I got up unscathed! As I age, I can barely take out the garbage without getting hurt. As a youth, I could be hoisted six feet into the air and land on concrete with no ill effects.

The second episode of "lead paint mind lapse when starting the Enfield" was a near carbon copy of the first. I went through the whole starting procedure, again forgetting to retard the spark, with nearly identical results. This time, as the engine backfired, rather than hoisting me into the air, the kick-starter ripped the heel off my engineer's boot and threw *it* into the air. The whole event occurred as if in slow motion. I remember my foot coming off the kick-starter and seeing the heel of my shoe shoot skyward. I assumed the airport radar in Bismarck picked it up as an unidentified flying object over the farm. I imagined the news reports.

"A heel-shaped UFO has been spotted near Arena, North Dakota. Radar reports the object entered the atmosphere at an incredible speed. Officials are on the way to the site of the wreckage to check for survivors and alien lifeforms. The Governor has put the National Guard on Alert."

The ripped-out heel bottom landed with a light thump in the grass beside me. I picked it up and examined it. Its surface was a mess of nails. The paranormal investigators weren't going to get their hands on this heel, no matter how much they threatened me. I needed footwear. I went to the shop and re-nailed the heel to my shoe.

The engine-starting mishaps reinforced my desire to get a modern motorcycle before the Enfield could break my leg. The agreement with my parents, to upgrade the Enfield to a Honda, was the right decision. However, little did I know that parent-child contracts could be changed unilaterally without the child's consent. Disappointments were to strike again.

CHAPTER 23
SOME FUN, STRENGTH TRAINING
& LOTS OF EMOTIONAL PAIN

The summer progressed, and so did the crops. We assumed it would be another fantastic harvest. Dad was so impressed with my rock-picking skills he decided it was time to purchase a new plow. For once, he had correctly reasoned that a *new* piece of equipment would speed things up. He went further into debt to buy a new John Deere trip beam plow. The trip beam plow was the first significant improvement to moldboard plows since John Deere fashioned the plow from steel in 1837. Before Deere's invention, wood or cast iron materials were used to manufacture plows. The sticky, heavy black soils of the American midwest stuck to those plows and often needed cleaning. The new steel plows were scoured, creating a shiny surface that didn't need cleaning. Another benefit was that they required less horsepower to pull so the same tractor could pull more plow bottoms. In the sixties, plows were re-designed to include a revolutionary trip beam feature. If the plow hit a rock, the individual plow moldboard bottom would release and rotate backward up over the rock. The operator would reverse to reset the plow and then continue forward. These improvements eliminated the need to carry a jack to raise the plow over the offending rock or rocks. The new plow was also designed to use hydraulics, another huge improvement from the old mechanical lift systems. Later on, further improvements to the trip beam design included springs that automatically reset the moldboard. Today, modern farm implements like the cultivator have primarily replaced moldboard plows.

The new plow was a considerable advancement over the old implement. During the summer I managed to plow up the forty new acres that I thought I had cleaned of rocks. After plowing, thousands of hidden rocks appeared that were buried slightly below the surface. I went back to picking rocks late into the fall and early the next spring to get the land ready for its first seeding.

I often went riding on the Enfield, not far, but, far enough to invoke the British Gods of Asylum Engineering. The Enfield engine was a good starter at home, but as the distance from our yard increased, the likelihood that the Enfield would start, or remain running, would decrease. I might've put more miles on the odometer by pushing it than I did by riding it.

Over tea and crumpets, I could imagine the designers at the asylum sitting around a table discussing how to make the Enfield a dual-purpose bike. The chief lunatic came up with the winning idea—*it could be a motorcycle AND a strength training machine!* It was rather poor at the former and excelled at the latter. The asylum advertising department could promote its fuel efficiency, proudly flaunting that it "uses no gas on your return trip!"

After a year of riding and pushing the Enfield home, the muscles in my legs had developed to the size of small trees. By my sophomore year, I excelled at high jump, long jump, and could dunk a basketball. I would've also won the rock-throwing competition, but it was not a sanctioned high school event.

North Dakota gets a bad rap about its weather. Depending on the season and which side of the state you're on, the climate varies. The western side is drier and has milder winters than the eastern side. Overall, the weather has extremes punctuated by days of beautiful blue skies, clean, crisp air, and moderate temperatures. Some of the recorded extremes are VERY extreme. In 1936, Steele, North Dakota, registered a temperature of one hundred twenty-one degrees while, in the same year, Parshall, North Dakota recorded a temperature of sixty degrees below zero; a difference of over one hundred eighty degrees! Lucky us; the location of our farm was between Steele and Parshall, so we were also subjected to these extremes.

The late fifties were very dry. In 1960, the drought broke, and our farm received over ten inches of rain in less than two hours. Because the rain gauge only held six inches of water, Mom, the weather fanatic, had to run outside to empty it in the middle of the storm. The resulting flooding washed out roads and swamped farmers' homesteads.

1964 began cool and wet but, by July, it was sweltering. As the daily temperatures approached or exceeded one hundred degrees, Dad would furrow his brow and comment on the possibility of hail. Buying insurance was way out of Dad's character, but thank goodness he did. Just as the crops were ripening for harvest, tragedy struck.

The morning was chilly and rapidly changed to a hot, humid day. On muggy days like this, the farm dogs would jump in the cattle water tank and then lay in the shade to cool off. By noon, the temperature was over one hundred degrees. At the time, air conditioners were rare, and people learned to cope with the heat the best they could. We had the good sense to stay in the cold basement.

North Dakota thunderstorms are magnificent. At about two in the afternoon, giant thunderhead clouds began appearing above the hills to the west of the farm. These clouds towered high into the sky with swirling shapes and colors of green, gray, purple, and black. Soon, we could see the lightning dance across the sky and hear thundering booms. From the safety of our living room, we witnessed white hail streaks in the clouds, ready to fall from the heavens. The air got eerily quiet for a moment, and then the wind hit with a force that nearly blew the house off the foundation. Within minutes, the hot and humid weather changed. The temperature dropped, and it was cold. Gigantic raindrops came crashing down, then mushy mixtures of rain and ice turned to hail. The hail battering the roof and clattering against the windows was terrifying! In thirty minutes it was all over. The storm had passed. As we emerged from the house, a startling site filled our eyes. Three inches of golf-ball-size hail blanketed the ground. The countryside looked like Christmas in July. The hail pellets had stripped the trees of their leaves and pounded the paint off the farm buildings.

After the storm, Dad and I waited for the creeks to stop running and then drove the pickup out to the fields to check the damage. The crops were flattened, so there would be no grain harvest, but, miraculously, the storm missed the cows in the pasture!

The hail insurance Dad had purchased was enough to cover our expenses for the year, but not enough for my parents to follow through on our deal of trading up to a new Honda. I would have to wait another year and experience yet another emotional letdown. By the age of fourteen, I had experienced enough character building to supply a small city.

CHAPTER 24
FIRE!

1965 looked promising. Even with the addition of forty new rock-picked acres, pleasant spring weather allowed me to be done planting by mid-May. I set a goal of removing the rocks from another forty acres and picked whenever time permitted.

Mom and Dad agreed to extend our contract from the previous year but, this year, I would hedge my bets. Instead of relying on the validity of the contract with my parents as my sole source of income, I chose to raise a 4-H steer. 4-H encouraged kids to raise livestock. They would have fall judging competitions and award Blue, Red, or White Ribbons to students with the finest projects. I took out a loan from my parents and agreed to repay them one hundred dollars for the steer when I sold it at the 4-H auction in the fall. If the steer I raised became a Blue Ribbon winner, I would be paid anywhere from five hundred dollars to one thousand dollars.

To city dwellers, life on the prairie might seem boring and dull, but I found it thrilling. Friends and family used any excuse to get together and visit. We had church outings at least once a week. There were card parties, 4-H clubs, birthday parties, bake sales, auction sales, softball and volleyball parties, school plays and much, much more. These activities brought communities together to celebrate and enjoy life. If a farmer became sick or disabled, the neighbors would unite to plant or harvest the crops. We worked as a team to make sure everyone felt they were part of something bigger. We needed each other to survive.

My favorite form of family entertainment was to visit relatives after they'd returned from their vacations. Our family didn't go on "vacations." We had milk cows. Seeing other parts of the world required living vicariously through our family tree.

Mom's oldest brother was also named Art. He and his wife, Ethel, lived in Roseburg, Oregon. As they traveled throughout the west, they took tons of pictures. Mom's younger brother, Bern, and his wife, Ruth, who lived on a farm one mile from ours, also traveled the country. The families would gather, usually at Bern's farm, to gaze upon what wonders of the world they had captured on film.

A group of the cousins would sit on the living room floor while the adults sat scattered on various types of furniture. While one of my uncles set up the slide projector, the adults would discuss the advantages and disadvantages of Kodacolor versus Ektachrome film. The type of film didn't matter to me. I thought all the pictures were fantastic—*they were in color!*

The photographer would narrate to us what the picture was about, where it was taken, why it was taken and otherwise inform the audience. I witnessed slides of the most wonderful scenes I had ever laid eyes on! There were pictures of the Space Needle and the unbelievable sights inside national parks like Yellowstone, Yosemite, and CanyonLands. I saw trees so big they had tunnels you could drive cars through! It was magnificent! Looking at these destinations was exhilarating compared to the lame family movies my dad and uncles made. These landscapes made my heart sing! When I got older, I pledged to see the world.

Our family also hosted visitors. People would unexpectedly show up at the front door to visit in the evenings, and I was often asked to give rides on the Enfield. Uncles, aunts, cousins, and acquaintances; everyone got rides. The motorcycle was a big hit. I made short trips to avoid invoking the Enfield's propensity for breaking down too far from home. I'd go down the driveway, around the turn, and take the straightaway to Buller's farm and back. That was enough of a ride to satisfy most of the relatives.

One summer evening, the Otto and Delia Brose family showed up for a visit. Otto was my Dad's Uncle and owned Brose Repair in Wing. He sold gas and repaired everything from lawnmowers and cars to tractors and combines. His shop was on the corner of two intersecting streets and was a local hangout for men of the area to tell tales and drink a beer from the bar next door. During one of these informal get-togethers a jerk neighbor, whom we shall refer to as "Mr. K," was in his usual drunken state, boasting and telling tall tales. Although he thought he was a regular comedian, the rest of the community didn't think so. As we were listening to Mr. K drone on and on, Dad's brother, Art, pulled up in his brand new, long, shiny, black Chrysler Newport Wagon. It was glistening. Art had moved to Bismarck and required the station wagon as part of his job. As he exited the car, Mr. K attempted to demean him in front of the others by yelling out, "HA! IT LOOKS LIKE A HEARSE!"

Mr. K had chosen the wrong person to ridicule.

Art had a rapier wit and immediately replied, "Yes, it does look like a hearse, and if you make any more comments, you'll be my first customer."

Mr. K's face quickly went blank, and he looked like he was afraid to swallow the beer in his mouth. The other men broke into uproarious laughter. Mr. K left the scene humiliated.

Otto and my Dad were almost the same age, so it happened that Otto and Delia's kids were around the same ages as my sisters and I. We called them cousins even though they were technically "first cousins once removed." Leland was one year my senior and Bradley was two years my junior. We were all good friends. While Otto and Delia went into the house to visit, Bradley, Leland, and I went to ride the Enfield.

They were excited about their first opportunity to ride a motorcycle. I went through the usual starting routine without success. The Enfield refused to start. Its gas tank was almost empty, and I reasoned by filling the tank, I might improve the odds of getting the beast running. I pushed it to the over to our three-hundred-gallon gasoline dispensary and used the nozzle to fill the Enfield's tank. After a few more attempts at starting, I concluded that the spark plug had fouled. From years earlier, I remembered watching Uncle Art and Dad's process to get Art's Harley running. I walked to the shop for a spark-plug wrench. When I removed the plug, it was wet with raw gasoline so, I heated the end with a propane torch to dry it out. I replaced the plug and resumed the starting procedure. At the first kick, catastrophe struck. The engine did not backfire, but a jet of fire shot out the air inlet of the carburetor. At first, a small flame consumed the gasoline in the carburetor, but then the fire rapidly advanced, burning holes in the plastic gas lines. Soon, a conflagration was raging next to our three-hundred-gallon gasoline tank! A perilous situation was threatening to burn down the whole family farm! At this point, the motorcycle was irrelevant. We needed to stop the fire before it spread to the gasoline storage tank and the farm buildings.

Leland ran to the house to tell the adults what was happening. I ran to the barn and filled two five-gallon pails with water from the cattle water tank. As I was lugging the buckets of water over to the gasoline tank, Otto had exited the house and ran to his Dodge car. He kept a fire extinguisher in the car and was coming to my rescue. Unfortunately, to get to the motorcycle, he had to run around a giant cottonwood tree in our front yard. Mom would often water the tree with a garden hose to keep it healthy. Otto was unaware the ground was saturated, and as he rounded the corner at breakneck speed, he lost his footing on the muddy clay. His right foot started sliding out from under him, and he began going down. Using the fire extinguisher in his left hand, Otto attempted to counter the fall. When his body was at about a forty-five-degree angle to the ground, he involuntarily pulled the handle of the extinguisher. We watched as it shot a giant arc of white foam across the sky, reminding me of big, billowy clouds. From my viewpoint, it was all very comical. As the foam landed in piles around the yard, I arrived at the motorcycle with the pails of water. Otto had regained his footing. He waved me away from the inferno and aimed the extinguisher. He pulled the trigger, and the extinguisher went, "phit."

A small dollop of foam, what looked like a scoop of ice cream, exited the fire extinguisher and landed on Otto's shoe. He'd accidentally emptied the extinguisher when he fell rounding the cottonwood. The small blob was all that was left. At that moment, the situation was funnier than it should've been. We were watching fire consume the Enfield, and I was on the verge of laughing out loud. I regained my composure and dumped a pail of water on the fire with good results. The second pail almost entirely extinguished the blaze. As I ran back to the water tank, Bradley arrived at the scene with a bucket of his own. Otto grasped the pail and threw it on the Enfield, extinguishing the fire. We had successfully avoided a farm calamity, but the motorcycle was a total disaster.

I took a visual inventory of the damage. All the rubber parts were burned off, the aluminum controls on the handlebars had melted, the control cables were toast, the tires were charred, the battery was gone, the wire insulation was non-existent, the headlight and taillights were busted, the candle-wax turquoise paint job was crispy, and all the chrome parts had blued from the heat. The Enfield was in tough shape.

We dragged the motorcycle away from the gasoline storage tank to prevent it from re-igniting and went into the house to discuss the event. As we indulged on Mom's homemade strawberry shortcake, everyone chatted about the fire. Otto maintained that the fire extinguisher would have done the job if it weren't for his klutzy fall. Dad admonished me for trying to start the Enfield so close to the farm gas tank. Mom asked, "Does anyone want more strawberry shortcake?"

We all raised our hands.

At this point, I was jaded and had gotten used to continually having my religious beliefs tested. I no longer cried when faced with adversity. My tear ducts had dried up from overuse. I had a decision to make: abandon the Enfield, or plan to rebuild. I was still expecting locusts to fill the skies and frogs to rain down.

CHAPTER 25
THE LONG WAY BACK

The parts quote from Nicholson Brothers confirmed my worst fears. It was going to take almost two hundred and fifty dollars to buy new parts. In addition to the shipping and customs duty, the total would be closer to three hundred U.S. dollars. In the fall, my 4-H steer should sell for close to one thousand dollars, and after paying my parents for the steer, I could net as much as nine hundred dollars. If I sold the steer for anything over eight hundred dollars, I decided I would buy a brand new Honda. A 305 Scrambler was about eight hundred dollars and would be money well spent. I wouldn't have to waste any more money and time on rebuilding the burnt-out hulk that was once the Enfield. I decided to wait until fall to make a final decision. I occupied myself with rock picking, laying out new fields, making hay, and caring for "Rocky," my 4-H steer.

4-H clubs across America got kids involved in productive endeavors and improved self-worth. Each member had a project like crafting or science they would enter into the fall judging competition held in Bismarck. Most farm kids' projects involved livestock such as goats, sheep or cattle. The livestock was scored based upon the animal's physical condition, breed, temperament, and show. "Show" was the quality of how well the animal and its trainer worked together in front of the judges.

In the livestock sales barn, the contestants would walk around a ring while a judge called out commands. The 4-H member would then pull on their animal's halter, getting it to respond to the various inputs.

To show Rocky, I would need a halter. I spent twenty dollars on a fancy, red-leather halter fashioned by Larry's older brother, Leland. Leland was an artist of first-rate credentials. He could draw cartoons, create lifelike sketches and was super-handy. Leland excelled at leather work. He was making horse saddles in high school, and his products were in high-demand as Christmas gifts. His hands expertly crafted tooled leather purses, wallets, belts, and other goods. The halter he made for Rocky was masterful. It was a functional work of art.

The day of the judging had finally arrived. I had spent many hours with Rocky grooming him, adjusting his diet, teaching him to accept the halter and respond to commands. He was a nice-looking, well-behaved animal. However, I didn't know when I started the project, that to be the Blue Ribbon winner, the steer had to be from purebred beef stock, like Angus, or Hereford. Rocky had a Holstein bull for a father and a Hereford cow as his mother.

He was a crossbreed—doomed from the beginning! There was no way we could win the Blue Ribbon.

The livestock was housed in pens at the livestock barn the night before the event. Roger Koski lived on a farm several miles from ours. Roger was four years younger than me and was already a cattle mastermind. Their farm raised purebred cattle, and he had picked the best-of-the-best for his show steer. They placed his beast in a pen next to mine.

When you select a steer, you have no idea what temperament that steer will develop. When Roger picked his steer, he had unknowingly chosen poorly. His steer was a kicker. It would violently kick its rear legs at the slightest sound or motion. It was a hazard to the judges and other exhibitors. A veterinarian was on hand for the event, and he recommended a sedative to make the animal safer to handle. The judges agreed it would be for the best and the veterinarian administered the sedative with a hypodermic needle. The effect of the sedative was immediate and hilarious. Roger's steer still kicked, but, in slow motion. He would slowly raise a rear leg and extend it as if he was trying to shake hands. It was more of a greeting than a kick. All the exhibitors and judges gathered around Roger's pen to witness the transformation from flailing legs to a slow-motion hoof shake.

The next day we entered the arena with our steers. We went through the motions as directed by the judges. My crossbred steer won the Red Ribbon, and Roger's drugged steer received the Blue. When the judging was over, the auction began.

Local businesses were asked to support organizations like 4-H. Companies with philanthropic endeavors would send a buyer to bid on the livestock at above market values. In some years, steers had brought in as much as one thousand dollars! 1965 was not a normal year. Cattle prices were meager. A drought in the southern plains had caused southern ranchers to dump cattle on the market, to avoid feeding them through the winter. My steer sold for three hundred and eighty dollars, less than half of what I expected. Our 4-H leaders were shocked. I learned it was better to be in a business where I set the price, not the buyer. I went home with my money, knowing that I had to pay one hundred dollars to my parents for buying Rocky as a calf. I would only have two hundred and eighty dollars left in my nest egg. A new Honda was not in the picture unless Mom and Dad could honor the contract we had in place.

With very little to do on the long winter nights and our television on the fritz, I had become an avid reader. Eventually, I read nearly every book in the Wing School library, including the encyclopedias. Shortly after selling my steer, I was lying in bed reading *Sherlock Holmes: The Complete Novels and Stories* by Sir Arthur Conan Doyle. Dad entered my room with a solemn look on his face. My Sherlock Holmes observational powers kick-in. I knew the news was not good and braced for the worst.

"Son, I need your help. Sharon needs plane fare to get back from California, and I don't have any extra money. Will you loan me the money from your steer?"

My sister, Sharon, had married several years earlier. With the marriage strained, her husband, Jim, left her to live in California. At the beginning of the summer, she thought she could patch things up and had traveled to Los Angeles to be with him. The reunion was short-lived. Sharon called, pleading to come home. The Watts riots had broken out in Los Angeles, and she was afraid for her life. The city was burning down around their apartment. She needed airfare to get home—pronto.

Disappointments were nothing new. What was one more insult added to the pile? I agreed and handed over the money. I thought I had waved my motorcycle goodbye for another year.

They say, "good things come to those who wait." I had been waiting for years. Good things were about to happen.

CHAPTER 26
NO GOOD DEED

In my mind, the nest-egg money I handed to Dad, was as good as gone. I believed I would never see it again. It wasn't enough money to buy a new Honda, but it was enough to buy parts to fix the Enfield. I tried to forget about the money and concentrated on farming. The hailstorm had wrecked most of our grain crops, but the fields could be swathed and put up for hay. We had hay left over from the previous year, and now we would have twice the crop.

Mom and I made hay faster than Dad could bale it. We used bales, rather than stacks (loose piles). Even though stacks required less labor, bale transportation was more economical. Neatly baled hay could be loaded onto semi-trailer trucks and easily transferred to trains and cargo ships for international trade. In 1965, due to widespread drought, hay was in huge demand, and local and export prices were high. Dad sold the hay that fall and had more money than usual. The crops on our farm damaged by hail and made into hay ended up being worth more than the grain would've been. Mom and Dad were able to pay back my nest-egg loan but claimed they were unable to add any additional money to buy the Honda. Dad was scheming for a new project of his own.

It was a time of farming transition. Just a few years before I was born, local farmers were still farming with horses. When I was a toddler, our team of draft horses was still alive. I used to marvel at them, Tom and Jerry. They were monstrously large beasts. They were a breed called *Percherons*. Muscular, intelligent, and now old, Tom and Jerry had been retired to live the good life. As strong as the horses were, they were no match for modern tractors.

In 1948, Dad purchased a new International Harvester H. It was a good tractor for making hay or pulling a stone-boat but was too small for many farm jobs. When Dad bought the used International W-9 in the early fifties, he thought it would be the powerful, all-purpose tractor he needed. He was wrong. It lacked power steering, brakes, and hydraulics (I added hydraulics later). It had terrible ergonomics, was a gasoline guzzler, had poor visibility, and wasn't much more powerful than the smaller "H" tractor. We used the W-9 for one job—plowing. It was too clumsy for anything else. Initially, Dad thought he could use it to help clean up the rocks, but it wasn't the right tractor for the job. He'd always dreamed of owning a machine powerful enough to move rock piles and dirt. His dream was about to come true.

We lived in Burleigh County. It's about seventeen hundred square miles of hills, farms, towns, sloughs, creeks, and rivers. It had miles and miles of paved and unpaved roads. The county coordinated with their cities and townships to build and manage the roads. They had established regional shops to maintain and store the heavy equipment. Our nearest town, Wing, had a county shop. On the lot, for sale, was a pre-World War II Caterpillar D8 tractor and bulldozer the county was trading in for a new model. Dad used the money promised me, the extra cash from the hay sales, and a small loan from the local Caterpillar franchise, Schultz Machinery, to buy the old D8. He thought he got the deal of a lifetime-only eighteen hundred dollars. I believe Schultz Machinery was selling it for its scrap value. Perhaps they both got what they wanted.

On a Saturday I drove Dad to Wing so he could pick up the D8 and drive it home. Two hours later, Mom and I stood outside the house and watched as he pulled into the yard with his new-old toy. Having to sacrifice the purchase of my new motorcycle was worth it. He was beaming. He parked next to our little shop and jumped off the machine. He eagerly showed me the cable control unit used to raise and lower the dozer, the little gas engine which was used to start the big diesel engine, and the levers and brakes used for turning. It reminded me of building the Enfield.

CHAPTER 27
LIFE IN A TENT

Over the next few days, Dad loved his life. He used the D8 to push monster rocks off our fields and fix washed-out roads. During his earthmoving practice, he noticed the controls felt sloppy, and the engine misfired under load. An engine overhaul would be necessary before we could seriously use the D8.

Winter was fast approaching, and we had nowhere to work indoors on the D8. Another one of Dad's favorite places to shop was the Army Surplus store in Bismarck. Genuine military tires, shoes, engines and other miscellaneous items were mixed in with merchandise and hardware suitable for the local market. In one of the corners of the store, Dad noticed a new Army maintenance tent still in its wood crate. It looked like the perfect size! One hundred dollars later it was on its way to our farm. We parked the D8 a few feet from our small shop and quickly erected the tent over the top of the Caterpillar. The canvas tent was ideal. It would've been perfect for army field maintenance.

With the tent up and the D8 protected from the weather, it was time to start wrenching. Every day, Dad worked on the Caterpillar. I helped every night after school and on Saturdays. On Sundays, being dedicated Christian folk, we didn't work except for performing the essential milking and cattle feeding duties and reserved the remainder of the day for rest.

We soon realized our tools were far from adequate to work on heavy equipment like the D8. Our tool selection was barely sufficient to work on small farm machinery, much less the monstrously sized nuts, bolts, and pieces that were required to disassemble the Caterpillar. Dad assessed the problem. We need some monster wrenches, three-quarter inch drive sockets, a hoist to lift heavy parts, and a heater for the tent. Dad's Uncle Otto came to the rescue. He loaned Dad an old chain hoist, the monster-sized wrenches, and the sockets. During the next trip to the Army Surplus store, he bought a space heater that ran on kerosene and a mobile track onto which we could mount the hoist. We had enough tools to get to work.

The Caterpillar company headquarters is in Peoria, Illinois. Peoria must be *at least* one hundred miles from the nearest asylum, and their products reflect that sound decision. They have a world-class reputation as "the best of the best." Every detail is engineered and built to exacting standards. Our forty-year-old D8 was almost worn out, but we could still rebuild it. We could replace every worn pin and bushing. Every part was still available in Caterpillar's parts system. No asylum engineering here. There wasn't a Whitworth fastener in sight! It was and still is, a great American company.

We worked out a division of labor. I was in charge of rebuilding the controls and Dad was in charge of the engine. The D8 had lots of levers, linkages, and pedals. From its years of hard labor, every pin and bushing was worn out. As I disassembled all the items, I tallied a list of the parts that needed replacing; we'd use it to order the new parts. Dad's brother, Art, would help us on his days off. Dad and Art went after big game, the engine. It was exciting for them to work together again. They told stories and laughed as they removed each part from the engine, inspecting it through the smoke curling from their cigarettes.

Dad suspected a burnt valve was causing the misfire of the D8's monster, six-cylinder, diesel engine. Art attached the overhead chain hoist and started the process of lifting the heads off the engine. As soon as the second piston was exposed, he discovered the culprit.

Art said, "Ray, you've got a big problem."

The piston had a hole in its top. Upon inspection, almost all of the other aluminum piston tops were nearly burned through. Dad saw the pistons and panicked. This repair was not going to be a simple valve job. The engine now required a major overhaul. It was a significant setback. Dad's dream had quickly become a nightmare.

Dad took my list and added the new pistons, rings, rod bearings, piston pins, and valves required to rebuild the engine and headed for Bismarck. He apprehensively approached the Schultz parts counter, expecting bad news. The Caterpillar parts man went through the list, checking his inventory.

"We've got everything except the pistons, rings, and valves," he said.

Dad's face was forlorn. Without the pistons and rings, the D8 was just a lump of worthless steel. The parts man then added, "The other items can be here tomorrow, from Denver."

Dad's expression changed to glee.

"How much?" he asked as he blew a smoke ring in the air. The parts man added the total on his sheet.

"Thirteen hundred dollars," he replied.

"Okay, let's get everything ordered," Dad answered. The businessmen at Shultz Machinery had been very astute when selling the D8 to Dad. They had given him a line of credit to buy the D8 plus an additional twelve hundred dollar line of credit to buy parts. It was a win-win.

For Dad, after years of working with local farm-implement dealers who seldom had parts on hand, this was a whole new world! The Caterpillar dealer could get any part, for any Caterpillar machine— *overnight!* The next day, Art loaded his station wagon and brought the pieces out to our farm. We inspected the new parts and observed the pistons were different from the originals.

The D8 had a diesel engine. While operating, injection nozzles shot raw fuel into the combustion chamber. Unfortunately, the fuel injection nozzles sprayed directly at the center of the pistons. After forty years, the diesel had eroded a hole in the top of the pistons. The new pistons had a stainless-steel insert where the fuel hit the top of the piston.

Caterpillar had learned from years of experience and had made the necessary improvements to fix the problem. The "new" pistons would last forever.

We disassembled, rebuilt, and reassembled the D8 through the winter of 1965. Things were going splendidly. Soon, Dad was going to have his new toy, and I would get the shop back to start rebuilding the Enfield. I had ordered parts in December, and the boxes were waiting for my attention. Dad and I needed to hurry up and finish the D8 project so I would have the time and space to rebuild the motorcycle before spring.

CHAPTER 28
BLIZZARD!

The winter had been quite mild. By the first of March, we were thinking about sowing the fields. There had been little snow, and the temperatures were moderate.

On Tuesday, March 2, 1966, I was sitting in study hall at the Wing High School. Around one thirty, Superintendent Sorenson entered the classroom and hurriedly spoke.

"I have an announcement to make."

"*Oh no,*" I thought to myself, *"not another assassination."*

"The United States Weather Bureau has notified all schools in North Dakota, South Dakota, and Minnesota to close immediately. A massive storm is moving in from the Rockies and will strike our area within hours. Leave as soon as your bus arrives. Students driving cars are advised to stay in town until the storm is over. Check with my office for families with extra rooms for lodging. Students living in town are asked to go home immediately."

"Big deal," I thought sarcastically to myself. I had been through many blizzards before. I figured the teachers just wanted an excuse to get out early. Going home sounded like a great idea to me! I wanted to work on the Enfield.

We boarded the bus around two. The wind was lightly blowing out of the east, and the sun was a hazy gray to the west. It was not much of a "blizzard." About an hour later, around three, the bus stopped at one of its last stops, our house. The wind had switched to the northwest, and big snowflakes had begun to fall. Mom and Dad greeted me as I entered the house. They had heard the news of the impending storm and were making plans to protect our livestock. Mom and Dad would milk the cows and leave them in the barn. My job was to wrangle the range cattle into the various barns and lean-tos and then haul hay bales to each barn to provide them with feed, in case the storm lasted more than one night. The plan was a good one, and its implementation may have saved our farm from financial ruin.

We completed our chores around five thirty. By now, it was snowing heavily. Then, the wind struck with the ferocity of a tornado. Instant WHITE OUT! Dad suggested we link arms and walk to the house, some one-hundred-and-fifty-feet away, to avoid getting lost in the storm. As we exited the barn, an extraordinary blast of wind hit my face. Visibility was less than two feet. To find the house, we would have to try to walk a straight path perpendicular to the barn. It was going to be difficult. The storm had just started, and snow drifts were already two feet deep.

It took us ten minutes to walk to the house. On the way in, we sheltered the dogs in the garage and quickly opened the door to be greeted by the warmth and serenity of our new home. Miraculously, the electrical power was still on. Mom made a batch of homemade bread and vegetable soup to warm our frozen bodies. After supper, we watched the progress of the storm on the television. Locals would telephone into the weather service stations and report their observations. The weatherman was speechless as every reporting station in the area had the same reports of zero visibility, fifty-mile-per-hour winds, wind gusts up to seventy miles per hour and heavy snowfall.

Mom came into my room to say evening prayers. She asked God to keep the electricity running and to make sure everyone was safe through the storm. As I climbed into bed and drifted off to sleep, I was smug thinking officials would cancel school tomorrow, we could sleep in, and I could work on the Enfield after morning chores.

I awoke at seven the next morning to the wind screaming around the house. I could hear Mom and Dad talking in hushed tones in the living room. I walked to the living room and joined Mom and Dad looking out "the window," or what remained. The snow had drifted up the house about nine feet, obstructing our view. Through the intense snowfall, we could barely make out the big cottonwood in the front yard. It was nearly horizontal from the wind. We had gone to bed with winds *gusting* to seventy miles per hour. Now, the seventy-mile-per-hour winds were constant, *and* it was snowing at least an inch per hour! Mom said it was much too dangerous to go outside and Dad agreed. Milking and morning feeding would have to wait until the storm subsided. The Enfield would also have to wait.

Dad spent the day reading and napping. Mom and I played Chinese Checkers and Carrom. She made us buttered popcorn and hot chocolate as a treat. By mid-afternoon we had a decision to make—*do we risk our lives to milk the cows?*

By not milking, we were risking the health of our dairy cows. They should be milked twice a day. We had already missed morning milking so we decided we should try to perform the evening chores before sunset, to lessen the chance of getting lost and dying from exposure. We donned our chores' clothes, wrapped our faces with extra scarves, and linked arms, preparing to adventure towards the barn. The wind speed had declined slightly. Giant snow drifts surrounded us, and, as we began our lockstep, there, in front of us, was a miraculously cleaned path through the snow to the barn!

When we got to the barn, the cows were *very* happy to see us. I doubt any of them had thoughts of escaping to an open gate. While Mom and Dad finished milking, I fed the range cattle and carried water to the calves. Our cream separator required hot water for cleaning, and our only source of hot water was the house, so, Mom and I locked arms and trudged to the house and back to retrieve the five gallons of hot water required for washing up. Afterward, we all trudged back to the house together afraid we were living in a nightmare. It had been snowing for twenty-four hours, and it was storming worse now than when it started.

As we watched television that night, the local stations were reporting the storm was going to break tomorrow four hundred miles away in South Dakota. The winds were diminishing, and that weather was heading our way. We went to bed with renewed optimism that soon our lives would return to normal. As I closed my eyes in my fuchsia-painted, seventy-degree surroundings, I wondered if our old house would have survived the storm. While I fell asleep, I didn't care. It was becoming just a memory of my past.

Day three started just like day two. The storm was as strong as it was on day one. By ten the snow was falling in squalls, the winds remained at fifty miles per hour, and visibility was maybe ten feet. We performed our morning chores and returned to the safety of the house for another day of popcorn, hot chocolate, and games. Dad called his brothers in Bismarck. They reported the storm was intense, but some traffic had resumed in the city. After phoning the neighbors and discussing the conditions at their farms, he concluded we were in the middle of the worst part of the storm. We trudged out for evening chores and returned to the house following our linked-arm, lockstep routine. That night the local weather service in Bismarck said the storm had broken and gusty winds would remain throughout tomorrow. We endured another night of severe weather with prayers and wondered if the weathermen were right.

On the morning of day four, the weather had much improved. The winds were still gusting, but it had quit snowing. After over sixty hours of storming, snowbanks covered most of the windows. Dad tried to get out of the house, but the snow was blocking the doors. We worked to shovel out a tunnel and were shocked by the massive snow drift that was covering our house. White hills blanketed everything in sight.

As we walked toward the barn, that nearly snow-bare path remained from the house to the barn. *How could this have happened?* When we passed the giant snowbank covering our house, we saw the reason. The Army tent Dad had erected to enclose the D8 had blocked the wind and snow so that a barren patch of ground extended between the two buildings. Without pitching the tent in its precise location in the yard, we would've had a twenty-foot-deep drift blocking our path between the barn and the house. We may not have been able to survive our trips back and forth to do chores. It was like Moses parting the Red Sea, except this was an Army tent parting the "Blizzard of '66". As we moved closer, we could see the shelter had sacrificed its life to provide us safe passage. It was torn and mangled from the storm, although most of its canvas was still intact. It was a miracle!

After milking, the cows were happy to be let outside. They ran to the water tank to drink. After chores, we assessed the situation. We didn't own a Farmhand Loader attachment for the tractor. We had no suitable method to clean up the after-effects of the storm. With twenty-foot-high snowbanks towering for as far as the eye could see, our only option was a shovel. It appeared Hell had frozen over.

I turned to Dad and started mumbling about how it would take weeks to shovel all the snow. He grinned and pointed towards the Army tent. It was housing the D8. Dad and Art had worked feverishly to finish it up the day before the storm hit so Art could return to Bismarck and avoid getting snowed in at our farm. It hadn't been started since the overhaul, and now it was time to see if Dad's intuition and mechanical abilities would pay off.

We made our way to the tent. He opened the shredded remains of the flap door and inspected the interior. Some snow had covered the machine, and as I shoveled it away, he installed the "Comfort Cover." The Comfort Cover was a canvas cover that went over a metal framework creating an operator compartment that would trap heat from the engine. While operating the machine, the engine fan would blow engine heat into the compartment, keeping the operator warm.

Three days of cows in the barn made a disgusting mess. I offered to clean the barn as Dad bulldozed snow. Using a wheelbarrow and a pitchfork I figured I could finish in two hours. I was daydreaming that a gang of Klingon slaves would arrive to assist me when Dad asked me to help him start the D8. He was ready for the time of his life.

CHAPTER 29
SNOW MOUNTAINS

It was quite the procedure to start the D8. Dad drained any fluid from the gas-starting engine by opening a petcock on the combustion chamber. Then, he closed the petcock and turned on the gas valve from the small gasoline tank. He turned the magneto switch to "ON," applied the choke and set the throttle. After inserting the crank, he turned over the little gas engine. On the second try, it sputtered to life. The muffler-less exhaust sounded like machine-gun fire. Because the little gas engine shared coolant with the big engine, running the small engine would heat the big engine as well. He let the little engine help warm the big engine, and after a few minutes, he made sure the big engine compression release was open, engaged the starting engine clutch, and watched the big engine turn over. After a few seconds, he engaged the compression lever and the big diesel burst to life. It knocked furiously, as diesel engines do in the cold. Dad shut off the little gas-starting engine and climbed aboard his steed. He was beaming.

Soon after exiting the tent, he was dozing ten to twenty-foot-high snow drifts. Within an hour, our yard was clear of snow, and he began pushing the snow off our half-mile driveway, on the way to Buller's farm. As he approached, Uncle Dave, Larry's father, came running to meet Dad. The snowbanks were too big and packed too hard for his Farmhand Loader. He asked Dad to clear the snow from his yard. Dad agreed, and an hour later their yard was cleared. Then, Dave said he needed hay to feed his cows, and the haystacks were a half-mile away and blocked by snow.

Since I had finished cleaning our barns, Mom and I went to the Buller farm to watch the D8 in action. Dad started toward the stacks of hay in the distance. There were several snowbanks in the way that even the D8 could not break through. Instead of trying to break through the snowbanks, he drove over them! The tracks had so much surface area the machine could float over the snow like a toboggan!

As dad arrived at the haystacks, I thought, *"Now, what?"*

I assumed he would doze a path to the haystacks to provide Dave with access. Instead, Dad dropped the blade of the dozer behind a stack, engaged the clutch, and pushed the pile of hay over the snow to Dave's barn! It sure was simpler than hauling hay on my sled! Uncle Dave gave Dad fifty dollars for his two hours of work!

As Mom and I returned home, the phone was ringing. Martin Heidt, a neighbor, was on the line.

He had watched from a distance as Dad moved the snow at Buller's farm and asked if Dad could come right away to clear his yard and driveway. I hurried to the pickup and drove to tell Dad before he drove home with the D8. Something was happening. It was the beginning of something new. Dad never anticipated doing Caterpillar work for others. All of a sudden, he was thrown into a new profession, *cat skinner*. He loved it. By the time I returned home from Buller's, Mom had taken three more calls from local farmers needing Dad's services, and the phone was still ringing. Dad worked night and day for several weeks. After the major roads were clear of snow, Uncle Art came from Bismarck and took his turn running the D8. Between the two of them, the D8 ran twenty hours a day for the next month. It was a godsend to the local community and our income.

The aftereffects of the storm would remain as remnants of snow, well into the month of June. The snow had hardened, and the enormous snowbank behind our house offered terrific tobogganing. I'd seen surfing movies on television and thought, *"I could do that."*

I taught myself to toboggan standing upright, like an ocean surfer, sailing down the snowbanks like a modern-day snowboarder.

Marvin Wetzel would show up on his Honda CT90 Trail. We could shoot up one side of the snowbank and down the other on the little bike. Then, we tied a rope to it and used it as a mule to pull a rider on the toboggan. It was fun and exhilarating!

The magnitude of the storm's toll on area livestock and wildlife was devastating. As the snow melted, we found over forty dead pheasants that had frozen to death under a snowbank in our trees. The deer that survived the storm later risked being killed by starvation or being hit by cars. There were no places for them to walk or to feed. They could only follow the narrow trails created by the snowplows, which were also being traveled by cars and trucks.

We were fortunate we sheltered our cattle, but there were estimates that over one hundred forty thousand head of livestock suffered a cruel fate by the blizzard. Many died from exposure during the storm, and many more would die after from starvation and calving problems in the snow.

At least eleven people died from the effects of the storm. Our community was blessed. Our electrical power stayed on, and the temperatures never got below twenty degrees. No one was injured.

Thanks, Mom.

CHAPTER 30
IS THAT THE PHONE
OR ARE MY EARS RINGING?

The service demand for the D8 was overwhelming. The phone rang night and day. Farmers wanted snow moved, barn lots cleaned, rocks buried, and stock dams built. There was a constant and overwhelming need for what Dad could provide. Dad had hit a Grand Slam. During the snowmelt, as Dad and Uncle Art worked shifts running the D8, Mom and I performed the chores and looked for our farm equipment that had gone missing under the blanket of snow. The swather, combine, grain auger, and plow were all covered. By mid-March, a few items began to poke through the snow. The last implement to show itself was the grain auger. It was along the tree rows underneath the largest snowbank. As the snow melted and refroze at night, the accumulated weight was more than the auger could support, and it was flattened. I thought it was a goner but, later in the spring, Dad managed to do metal magic and rebuild it.

The snow-covered fields had put all farming on hold so, after school and on the weekends, I started rebuilding the Enfield. I asked Mom to stock up on mercurochrome and Band-Aids.

The second build of the Enfield went much faster than the first. I disassembled everything for painting. Most of the paint had burned off and what remained was easily removed with steel wool and sandpaper. My adventures with wild colors had subsided, and I figured, if I was going to trade it in, I should paint it a color that will appeal to the largest segment of the population.

I had been reading a book about the history of the Ford Motor Company. There was a whole chapter dedicated to Henry Ford's decision to paint cars black. If it worked for Henry, it should work for me. *"Useless reinventing a proven marketing strategy,"* I thought.

By 1966, I had discovered Krylon aerosol paint. My painting history was dubious, and the advertising made it sound like their product was fool-proof. Usually, fool-proof means that you can always find a bigger fool than what was proofed, which made me a prime candidate for testing their product. The paint can's instructions read, "Spray in multiple light coats to avoid runs."

This technique was certainly different from the method used to paint the barn with our sprayer. The method for barn painting was, "Spray as much paint as possible and damn the runs."

I followed the rattle-can instructions to the letter. When I completed the task, I was ecstatic. I had achieved a perfect high-gloss black finish, and no gasoline bath was required!

I finished the reassembly by late March. The Enfield ran well and looked great. The fire had blued the chrome parts, but I found a product called Blue Away that removed the discoloration. The new cables, tires, controls, and rubber parts made the Enfield look like a new motorcycle. The paint sparkled in the sun. I was hesitant to drive it, until I could trade it in for the Honda, afraid something terrible might happen to it. As it turned out, the summer was going to be super-busy, and I wouldn't have much time to ride.

The dozer business continued to be spectacular. Dad needed to keep the machine running as many hours as possible to meet the demand for his services. We were using the Studebaker truck that we used for hauling grain to haul individual five-gallon cans of diesel fuel back and forth to refill the D8. With a one-hundred-and-eighty-gallon tank, it took an incredible amount of manual labor, and time, to fill the beast. We needed to upgrade to a service vehicle capable of hauling fuel in a big tank. A truck that could haul steel cables, dozer parts, and other equipment. Dad put on his thinking cap and began scheming.

CHAPTER 31
THE FRANKENSTEIN FORD

It was a Friday. I got off the school bus and went into the house. Mom said, "Change your clothes and go to the garage. Dad has something he wants to show you."

I had visions of a new motorcycle in my head. As I entered the garage, a sight so outlandish met my eyes, that I thought it was a joke. Dad was working furiously on a 1962 Ford F-100 pickup.

"I didn't realize the Bismarck Trading Post sold vehicles," I thought to myself.

Dad had been to Schultz Machinery and saw the pickup parked in the corner of the lot. It had been a light-duty, parts-runner for the company. After being rolled in a ditch in Minot, North Dakota, the insurance company wrote it off as totaled. It was a complete mess. The body was bent, it had a twisted box, and the passenger side was concave. Dad looked at me and smiled.

"We have to get it fixed by Monday. Art is running the D8 for me this weekend, and he has to go back to Bismarck Sunday night."

I then expected him to laugh maniacally. Working twenty-hour days must have finally taken its toll. He must be hallucinating. One look at the pickup, and it was obvious it should never be driven on the highway again. We couldn't fix it by Monday.

"Britain isn't the only place that needs asylums," I thought silently.

"Isn't it wrecked?" I asked.

"Yes," he said, "that's why I got it for only five hundred dollars."

"Well, you just can't argue with that logic," I thought (being the guy who had just rebuilt a motorcycle that burned to the ground). It was apparent our genes ran deep, even the bad ones.

We worked like maniacs (true to the definition of "maniacs") that weekend. We removed the box, tried to straighten the body (as best we could), pounded out the caved-in roof, got the doors to kind-of work (by using ropes to tie them shut), replaced the windshield, and installed the new head and tail lights. We violated the sanctity of observing Sunday as a non-work day (Dad was becoming more of a capitalist and less of a Democrat), and by Sunday afternoon, we had pieced it back together. Now, Dad pulled out all the stops- he said he was going to paint it.

"We can't leave it looking like this," he said.

I brought up the fact it was a *TOTALED* pickup and thought, *"What exactly should it look like?"*

Dad was adamant that without new paint, it wasn't suitable to drive. The metalwork was creased, and after pounding it out with hammers, patches of the original paint were missing.

"What color?" I asked.

"Well, it's already yellow, and all I've got for paint is CAT yellow, so that's what it will be," he answered.

Of course, the yellows were as different as night and day, but we were on a timeline to finish by Monday morning. Matching color palettes was not an option. Dad fired up the Drip-Master 5000 paint sprayer and hosed down the little truck with a coat of the yellow Caterpillar paint. If the turquoise Enfield paint job was the worst paint job in history, then the yellow Ford was a close second, maybe even a tie. If you tried, you couldn't have matched the runs, drips, and fisheyes exhibited. I thought, *"Maybe rust and dents would look better."*

As Dad finished, he said, "That should do it," and turned off the paint sprayer. As the yellow fog in the shop started to dissipate, he lit a Lucky, cocked his head to one side and admired his work.

"If this D8-farming-ranching-haying-milking-carpentry thing doesn't work out, Dad could work for Earl Scheib's body shop as a painter! He already had a sprayer!" I thought sarcastically.

The newly-painted pickup required several days to dry, although driving it before allowing the paint to harden may have improved the appearance. When Dad had some free moments, he painted the grill and bumpers white. On Wednesday, we backed it out of the garage into the sunlight for a test drive.

Frank Gehry is a famous architect that makes outlandishly designed buildings. I guess some people find buildings that look like a crashed Boeing 747 jetliner appealing. I find them to be ugly and non-functional. The little Ford F-100 exercised similar emotions. It was a Gehry masterpiece. Sitting there in the sun it still looked like a wrecked pickup, only now it looked like a wrecked pickup with an awful paint job. If one drew an imaginary line through the middle of the pickup between the front and the back, then the hood and front of the truck would point to the right while the box pointed to the left. The left-front side of the box was also higher than the right-rear side. This pickup was the perfect vehicle to park in a Gehry-designed garage.

With the time restrictions, dad had attempted to paint around the windows the best he could without masking, covering them in overspray. The world took on a yellow hue as passengers viewed their surroundings from the cab. Over the next few weeks, I used a wood chisel to scrape away the overspray.

The driving experience was akin to a controlled crash. As the driver steered the vehicle along the road in a straight line, the skewed front end suggested a hard right-hand turn was in progress. While looking in the rear-view mirror, the box indicated the pickup was headed left, into the ditch. It made me nauseous to drive.

Some days later we added a fuel service tank to the bed of the pickup. It held one hundred fifty gallons of fuel and, when it was full, the weight overwhelmed the rear springs of the little truck. The back end would squat, while the front end would become light-as-a-feather and rise. When driving over slight bumps, the front tires would lift off the ground. Watching from a distance, it must have appeared as an optical illusion, going two, maybe three directions at once. It would've been an awesome hippie vehicle, it could've easily won first place at a carnival freak show, and it should've been heralded as the greatest piece of abstract art of all time!

This aberration was the most dangerous, uncomfortable, hideous, underpowered service vehicle in history and it had cost only five hundred dollars. Now, it all made sense.

CHAPTER 32
BINGE SPENDING

In just three months the money made by the D8 made an enormous difference in our lives. Dad had grown up poor. Economically, my sixteen years on earth had not been much better. We weren't rich but, the future looked incredibly good. For the first time in my life, and certainly my parents' lives, we had the dream of economic security. Dad's optimism was at an all-time high, and he was going to spend money to make money.

Schultz Machinery had replaced The Bismarck Trading Post as Dad's store of choice. During a parts visit, he spotted yet another item of machinery that had been traded-in and looked lonely. There, in the corner of the lot, was an early 1950's D4 excavator. It was in the same corner where he had spotted Frankentruck. By this time, I was sure it was the location the dealership parked items slated for scrap.

The excavator had a decent bucket and hydraulic controls. It was worn out but, being a Caterpillar design, we knew we could rebuild it. Dad now had good credit at Schultz's, and after signing a $2,500 note, it was loaded into Orvin Buchholz's semi-trailer truck cattle trailer and transported to our farm. We didn't have an unloading ramp at our farm, so Orvin backed up to the steep ditch south of the house and Dad drove his new toy out of the trailer.

At the time of purchase, the salesman mentioned the D4 hydraulics were shot and needed rebuilding. Dad had talked to the service manager and purchased the parts required to fix the hydraulics. After rebuilding the pump with new seals, wear plates, bearings, and vanes the hydraulics were good as new. With the D4 Dad could load gravel at county gravel pits, while Art could run other jobs simultaneously with the D8. Because he had worked for the United States Department of Agriculture for many years, Art had accumulated months of "time off" to use for side-jobs. The statement, "Double your pleasure, double your income," seemed appropriate when talking about the Hinkel brothers, Art and Ray.

Thinking and planning were more comfortable with capital available to aid decision-making. The next piece of equipment Dad invested in was a 1956 International five-ton dump truck. It was a perfect match for the D4. Now, he could load a truck with gravel and haul it for the county to local roads, or to farmers that were graveling their private drives. With its hydraulic box, we could also use it to haul rocks. The truck and D4 would also be used after the next blizzard to clear snow out of yards and off roads.

The massive amount of blizzard snow made it look like spring farming would be delayed—a lot. The new farmland that was clear of rocks, in addition to the original land, would need plowing and seeding as soon as conditions allowed. By mid-May, the sloughs were at full capacity, and the fields were soaked and untillable. It looked like farming would not start until the first week of June, which is normally the end of planting. By the middle of June, it would already be the haying season!

Our school was out, and Dad said, "Let's go to Zerr's."

Zerr's Implement in Tuttle, ND was the Case Dealership for the area. Even though it was a small dealership, it stocked a wide-ranging selection of agricultural equipment.

We pulled up in our yellow "Abstract Art" Frankenstein pickup and viewed rows of new and used tractors, combines and implements. Freddy Zerr, the proprietor, came out of the office and greeted us as we admired the tractors on the lot. Freddy and Dad had known each other their whole lives. Freddy was a straight shooter and Dad expected unbiased advice when he asked for a good tractor to replace the W-9.

"*Any* tractor could replace the W-9," Freddy laughed. "How many bottoms do you pull?"

"Four? Maybe five?" Dad responded.

"New, or used?" asked Freddy.

Dad replied, "Well, these new ones are nice, but I doubt I can afford one."

Freddy answered, "A used one is half the price of a new one but, a new one includes a warranty and Case financing."

"What's Case financing?" asked Dad.

"Three months no interest and no money down," replied Freddy.

Fifteen minutes later Dad had signed on the dotted line for a new Case 730 diesel Case tractor with the "Case-O-Matic" transmission. The D8 had changed Dad into a diesel man. At $4,500, it was the largest investment, other than the new house, Dad had ever made. The favorable financing terms made it too good to refuse.

Two weeks later, the plow was hooked up to the new tractor. The old "H" didn't have a live power take-off (PTO) so, every time the operator pushed in the clutch, the mower would stop. The new Case had live PTO and hydraulics (meaning they worked even if the clutch was dis-engaged) and I couldn't wait to get started. I began plowing on the driest field first to avoid getting stuck. Farming had suddenly gone from a mundane exercise in pain management to something that was fun, exciting, and might even be considered enjoyable! It might even be considered more enjoyable than riding a new motorcycle!

By mid-June, the crops were all planted, and it was time to start haying. Our sickle mower used for haying was something slightly more advanced than a scythe. I was sure it was designed prior to World War II by the same team that had designed Whitworth fasteners. It was heavy, clumsy, unbalanced, and came with a long handle that required the operator manually lift the cutter bar over rocks and badger holes. It was designed to bolt directly to the hitch of an "M" or "H" International tractor. With a selection of various assisting-jacks, Dad and I would wrestle it into position on the tractor drawbar. Once attached, it would vibrate and shake itself apart. The system was not ideal, and since our Case 730 had live PTO, ideal for mowing, we now needed a new mower to match the capabilities of the new tractor.

Dad's sister, Arlene, had married Ernest Ulm. When they first married, they lived in Chicago, Illinois. Ernest was a Mechanical Engineer who possessed great abilities. I looked up to him as a role model. "Uncle Ernie" had had a magnificent career. While employed at the United Rubber and Tire Machinery Corporation, he helped invent the machinery to produce radial tires in the United States. Later on, he became the Chief Engineer at Monsanto Corporation. However, Ernie's early career was working for International Harvester and, in the late 1950's, Ernie and his team had invented the trailer type sickle mower (later copied by other manufacturers). The mower could now be hooked up as easy as a regular trailer! Another trip to Tuttle in Frankentruck would result in a brand-new, Case trailer type sickle mower. Not only was it easy to hook up, but it also ran as smooth as silk. The old mower shook wildly at full speed, so much so, it appeared as a blur behind the tractor. The new mower was actually visible when in use!

Before the summer was out, Dad also bought a new, twelve-foot Case digger (which I used every chance I had to clean more ground of rocks). It was mated perfectly to the "730" and its "Case-O-Matic" transmission. I could ease a digger tooth up on a buried rock, and then I could increase engine speed until the tractor would slowly advance, pulling the rock out of the ground. The tractor was powerful enough to pull out the rocks, but the force wasn't powerful enough to bend the digger tines, so it was an excellent match for our purposes. It was fast, efficient, and didn't require log chains, crowbars, or human effort. Dad could handle the bigger rocks with the D4 bucket, and we hauled the rest with the dump truck to the nearest rock pile.

In July, a new hay wagon with a hydraulic lift was purchased to haul bales home from the hay fields. We would load it with about one hundred bails, drive home, and then dump the bales in rows next to the feedlot. To unload the bales, we'd put a log chain around the bottom row of bales, tighten the chain with a wire stretcher, raise the bed hydraulically, and drive away. The bales would slide off the trailer and in five minutes we could do what used to take two hours! Because it was a four-wheel trailer, it took several attempts at backing-up to learn how to control where it was going. The power steering and brakes of the new Case 730 helped tremendously! Eventually, I got very skilled at backing it up squarely to the last load. I've never feared driving or backing up anything since. Being put through "Farming Boot Camp," I had acquired two of the most critical skills all good farmers learn-stubbornness and backing four-wheel trailers.

By late summer, the crops were ripening, and we were preparing for combining. Our old Cockshutt combine was on its last legs. Parts had become difficult to acquire, and working on it was a pain. It became apparent that welding and wire wouldn't be able to hold it together through another season.

One of my jobs on the farm was to get our oats made into ground oats, making them more easily digestible for the cattle. This process required shoveling the back of the Studebaker truck full of oats, driving to the Tuttle Mill and Elevator, getting the oats ground, and hauling them back home. We fed the ground oats to the milk cows and once a month, I needed to repeat the process to replenish our stock. It just so happened that one of the four roads in Tuttle, on the way to the elevator, went right past Zerr's implement. While driving by, I noticed several new and used combines on the lot. On the way out of town, I stopped and looked at the inventory. By now, Freddy recognized me as "Dwight Hinkel, Son of Ray, and the four-wheel-trailer-backing-legend" and he strolled out to meet me. The new combines were lined up in a long row, and one on the end of the row looked out of place. It was a little dusty and had some worn paint.

"Why is that combine in this row?" I asked Freddy.

"That one is last year's demonstration model, so it's been used. If you're interested, Case will let me sell it with the warranty, Case financing *and* its twenty percent off," he answered.

"Why hasn't it sold?"

"It was parked out at my farm. I just put it on the sales row this morning," Freddy replied.

"Would you hold it until I talk to Dad?"

He smiled and said, "Sure, I'll hold it until I hear from Ray."

At supper that night, I told Dad of my discovery.

"How much is it?" he asked.

In my enthusiasm, I had forgotten to ask the price. Dad looked interested and said, "I'm doing some work with the D8 near Tuttle. I'll stop by in the morning and talk to Freddy."

Dad hated working on the rickety Cockshutt combine. To gain access to the most crucial parts that most often broke or needed repair (buried under the beast), you had to be a circus performer and contort yourself into a pretzel. Since the Ringling Brothers Circus did not perform at our farm (even though Frankentruck would have been a major attraction), Dad was left to perform these feats by himself. I knew as soon as I mentioned the Case opportunity, that Dad was bitten by "new combine fever." Two days later, a semi-trailer truck pulled up to deliver our "new" Case 600 combine. I never did find out the cost, but I'm sure Dad figured he could earn more money running the dozer than he would've curled up inside the combine as a contortionist.

The demand for earthmoving jobs continued to grow. Dad had enough appointments booked to last the next two years. He was going to need more equipment.

A scraper is an implement pulled behind a tractor that fills with earth as the bottom drags along the ground. After filling the scraper bowl is full, the operator closes the apron (using hydraulics or cables), and transports the earth to the dump site. Using a scraper was much more efficient than trying to push the ground with a dozer over long distances.

Many of our new customers needed livestock dams for their cattle, horses or sheep. In the spring, after the snowmelt, small creeks flowed throughout the county but, by midsummer, that water had dried up. Not only would the dams stock enough drinking water for livestock for the duration of the summer and fall, but they were also a boon to local wildlife. A scraper, pulled by the D8, would be more effective than a bulldozer for building the livestock dams. During the 1950s, earthmoving equipment had changed from cable to hydraulic controlled. Since the D8 was cable-controlled, we needed an older, cable-operated scraper.

Dad began his search. The McIntosh County Shop, in Ashley, North Dakota, had a LeTourneau type "LS" scraper for sale. Of course, Dad bought it. Ashley was about two hundred miles away. How would we get it home? Towing it behind a regular farm tractor would take days! A semi-trailer truck *lowboy* could do the haul in hours but, those contractors were expensive to hire and had to be scheduled weeks in advance. An alternative transport method was needed.

CHAPTER 33
KEEP ON TRUCKIN'

When we purchased the D4, Dad had hired Orvin Bucholz to haul it home from Bismarck. Orvin owned a trucking company, lived only four miles from our farm, and usually hauled cattle to market in his semi-trailer truck cattle trailer. He was the same age as my deceased brother, and my Dad had taken him under his wing. Dad called Orvin and explained the situation of needing a method to haul home the scraper. Orvin had no way of hauling it, but he suggested he might be able to tow it behind his semi-truck tractor. They set a date for the attempt.

It would be a long day. The trip to Ashley would take at least five hours. Once we got there, it would take time to attach the scraper to the truck and then it would be another six-to-eight hour drive to return home. Since the scraper didn't have any lights, we needed to be off the roads by dusk. An early start would be required.

Orvin drove into our yard at four thirty in the morning. Dad and I climbed up into the cab with our water jug, a Thermos of hot coffee, and a lunch pail full of sandwiches and cookies. I brought along some comic books, *Mad* magazines and a new issue of *Cycle World* to occupy my time. As we drove east down our driveway, the rising sun illuminated a thin yellow line on the horizon. It would be up in less than thirty minutes. The temperature was rising, and it had already reached seventy degrees. Today was going to be hot!

The aging Ford semi-trailer truck engine was LOUD. We needed to shout over it. The small cab wasn't air-conditioned, so the windows remained down to control the heat. I was relegated to sit in the center of the cab, sharing space with the two gear shift levers. Orvin was rowing through the gears as we went up and down the hills. It was like watching a magician's act as he depressed the clutch and shifted gears, sometimes moving both handles, to get the truck to perform. After a few hours, Dad opened the lunch pail and handed us each a bologna and mayonnaise sandwich. I finished my sandwich, got a cup of coffee and a cookie, and read about the potential motorcycles to be sold in 1967.

We arrived in Ashley around ten thirty. The temperature was already in the nineties, and it was humid. The shop was on the north side of town, just off the highway. As we drove into the McIntosh County Shop lot, we saw the scraper for the first time. It was huge! Orvin estimated it weighed about seven tons!

Orvin looked at Dad and said, "Ray, this is too big and heavy to tow."

Dad said, "It's not as heavy as a cattle trailer full of cows."

Orvin went on to explain how half the weight of a cattle trailer is normally placed on the fifth wheel of the semi-trailer truck by the tongue of the trailer you'd be hauling. The scraper was like a child's coaster wagon and had no brakes. Without being able to place its weight on the fifth wheel of the truck, the weight of the scraper would serve as a force that could push the truck when stopping or going down hills. It would be akin to a fifty-pound child pulling a five-hundred-pound wagon. The procedure would've been so hazardous that Orvin refused to tow it. A new plan was required to get the scraper home.

As Dad nervously chain-smoked Luckies, drank black coffee, and whispered incantations, Orvin circled the scraper. He devised a brilliant plan. He noticed the gooseneck of the scraper was the same height as the fifth wheel of his truck. If we removed the front axle, tongue, and wheel assembly of the scraper, we could mount the scraper's gooseneck directly to the fifth wheel of the truck. With half of the weight bearing down on the truck, we'd be able to transport the scraper safely, and he'd come back and get the front wheel assembly at another time.

Suddenly, Dad's attitude turned optimistic. He wholeheartedly agreed with Orvin. The scraper was parked outside, so they needed to pull it into the McIntosh County Shop for modification. The shop had a large overhead crane. A chain held up the gooseneck of the scraper while five or six people grabbed the tongue of the scraper's front wheel assembly and pulled it out of the way. Dad asked me to grease the wheels while he and Orvin got busy making an adapter to attach the scraper to the fifth wheel of the truck.

The shop foreman assigned me a helper named Albert. Albert was a rail-thin, chain-smoking man who was always as nervous as a cat in a thunderstorm. I checked out the button head grease fittings on the axles and asked Albert to get me a pail of grease and the button head grease gun. I tried to make small talk with him as I pumped grease into the wheel bearings and asked, "What's the population of Ashley?"

A "deer-in-headlights" expression swept over his face.

"Mostly Lutheran?" he stammered.

I thought he didn't hear me correctly, so I repeated the question.

"What's the population of Ashley?"

He shuffled his feet and a light suddenly shown in his eyes.

"Oh, *the population*, it's mostly German," he said.

At this point, I realized Albert was slower than most folk and, as such, he had been assigned a menial job assisting at the county shop. He had missed his potential. *In Britain, he could have been in charge of bolt design for the Royal Navy!*

Being the metal worker, Dad soon had a design in his head and began the task of fabricating the hitch adapter. Metal was cut with the acetylene torch and welded with an electric arc welder. As they feverishly worked, I went outside and strolled around the huge scraper. Parked behind it was its front wheel assembly. As I absorbed the details of its design, I noticed that the scraper had a rear hitch and parked beside it was the tongue of the front wheels. An idea flashed into my brain.

Why not attach the front wheel assembly to the back of the scraper, and tow the whole thing at once?

A second trip to get the front end wheel assembly would not be required.

I was a *GENIUS!*

I explained my epiphany to Dad and Orvin. They loved the idea, and we agreed that was what we'd do.

By three in the afternoon, we had the scraper attached to the fifth wheel of the truck and the wheel assembly attached to the back of the scraper. Before leaving, Orvin pulled out brake lights that attached magnetically to the scraper. Wires ran forward to the truck, and when Orvin tapped on the truck brakes, the lights were activated. Our return journey was ready to begin!

The temperature was at least one hundred and five degrees. Even with the windows open, the truck cab felt like an oven. Heat from the engine combined with the heat from the sun made the conditions nearly unbearable. We chugged along at breakneck speeds somewhere between twenty and thirty miles per hour. Everything was working great. Several hours later, we needed gasoline and pulled into a gas station in Napoleon. Dad asked if there was a good place to eat. The gas station attendant said the diner, just off the highway, had good burgers and was air-conditioned. Ten minutes later, we entered a cool oasis in the middle of the desert. It was a welcome break.

I ordered two hamburgers with raw onions, pickles, and a giant chocolate milkshake. Dad and Orvin ordered the same, but with a cup of coffee. We watched as the burgers sizzled on the grill and the waitresses plopped gigantic scoops of ice cream into big metal mixing cups, destined for the green shake-making machine.

"WHRRRZZZZZZ."

My stomach started growling in anticipation.

Our waitress poured the milkshakes into tall glasses and served them with the burgers. She set the excess shake mixtures on our table in their metal mixing cups. As we devoured our meal, we refilled our glasses from the metal tumblers. It was one of the best meals I've ever had.

We resumed the crawl home. Bismarck is on the western edge of the Central Time Zone. The midsummer sun sets around nine fifteen, with twilight lasting until around ten. At eight thirty, we were still two hours from home. Other than the brake light, the scraper had no legally required reflectors or lights. Without those after dark, it was illegal to be driving on public roads. Getting home before sundown was going to be a race. Orvin upped the speed of the semi-trailer truck. We reached our yard just as the twilight disappeared in the West. The scraper was home, and we were safe. Success!

CHAPTER 34
DOG DAYS

Dogs are vital animals on farms and ranches. Besides providing companionship, they work as alarm systems when strangers approach, keep varmints out of the farmyard, and herd livestock. Dad's dog was named Sandy. He must've been born a couple of years before I was born. He appeared to be a part-Collie, part-English Retriever mix. Good natured and loyal he had a serious flaw- he loved to chase cars and trucks as they entered or left our farmyard. About 1962, being old, or careless, or both, Sandy was run over by the school bus. He had broken bones, including several compound fractures in his legs. Dad carried him to the garage and placed him on some blankets. He tried to set the broken leg bones by putting splints on the fractures. The pain must have been intense but, Sandy didn't flinch as Dad tried to fix the wounded areas. We gently washed his abrasions and Sandy and my dog Bobby took turns licking the wounds. We carried water to Sandy's side and carefully petted him as he lapped up the water. On day two, he looked like he might rally to survive, but, by day three, the wounds started to smell, and by the morning of day four, Sandy was dead. The first dog tragedy was over.

Several years later, Larry and I were pedaling our bikes home from visiting Jimmy Heidt's farm. Our motorcycles were down for repair, and we were no longer bikers (at least not for the short-term). We took a shortcut through the old Lein schoolyard. While passing the steps to the school, we heard the sound of whining puppies. As we neared, we saw two abandoned puppies in the schoolyard that had taken refuge under the steps to the school. Larry took one, and I took the other, and we pedaled our way home.

My puppy was a female. Dad said pets' names should end in an "E" sound, so I named her Trixy. In addition to Trixy, I had my faithful dog, Bobby. I had gotten Bobby from Leslie Mehlhoff, as a puppy around seven years earlier. Bobby was a beautiful, purebred, black German Shepherd. Super-smart and friendly he would follow the tractor up and down the fields as I plowed. While plowing, worms and larvae were exposed, and the seagulls would swoop down to feast on the easy pickings. Bobby would make sure to chase the seagulls or mice as they presented themselves.

Trixy was a mixed-breed. She had a sweet nature, was kind, and obedient. She was a well-behaved puppy and grew into a medium-sized dog, about the size of a Beagle. Bobby and Trixy had a great time playing together.

Dad had always blamed the death of Lamb Chop and my bunny on the neighbor dog. He claimed the neighbor dog was visiting our farm because of Trixy. Once, the neighbor dog and Bobby got into a vicious fight. Bobby had parts of his face torn, but eventually, he healed and was almost as good as new.

Trixy had a small litter of puppies right after the "Blizzard of '66". They were two male furballs of delight. After opening their eyes and being weaned, we tried to find them good homes. Our neighbor, Johnny Roseneau, got one pup, but the other one, Charley, never found a new home. Charley was a free spirit. He was a runner with a short attention span. He'd chase gophers, birds, grasshoppers, or anything else that attracted his attention. After his unfruitful chases, he would collapse in the shade of the barn with his long, pink tongue hanging out of his mouth.

Shortly after the blizzard snowmelt, I got off the school bus to be greeted only by Trixy. Bobby and Trixy always met me as I got off the school bus and walked me to the house. It was strange that Bobby wasn't at her side. I walked into the house saw Mom and Dad drinking coffee in the kitchen. Dad summoned me.

"I have some bad news," he began, "that neighbor dog was here again, so I decided to do something. We are out of ammunition for the twenty-two, and all I could find was one sixteen-gauge shotgun shell. By the time I got outside the neighbor dog was gone, so I went to shoot Trixy, 'cause she's the reason for all the animal problems. When I pulled the trigger, Bobby jumped in front of Trixy. He was hurt really bad, and I had to beat him to death with a stick because we didn't have any more ammunition."

I went numb. I went to my room and had a good cry. At least my Dad was courageous enough to tell me the truth; however, the thought of him beating Bobby to death with a stick still haunts me.

Trixy had survived the ordeal and had given us new hope in Charley, as our replacement for Bobby. By mid-summer, Charley had grown into a teenage dog. He had long curly, reddish-brown fur, giant paws and was almost as large as Trixy. For him, chasing animals became an obsession. Chickens were his favorite targets. He would race toward them as they squawked and flew away. Charley followed in hot pursuit but, he was never fast enough to catch one. Then, it happened. At supper one night, Mom said she had watched Charley kill a chicken. Dad exploded in rage.

"WE CAN'T HAVE OUR DOGS KILLING OUR CHICKENS! ONE MORE INCIDENT AND CHARLEY WILL BE PUT DOWN!" Dad exclaimed.

I knew nothing about dog training. Teaching Charley to love chickens, at least live ones, would be a challenge. During the next few days, I would scold him whenever he got into a chicken chase. That had little effect on him. He would stare at me with a vacant look in his eyes. Soon, another tragedy happened.

Some years earlier, a mink decimated our chicken population when it got into the hen house and killed most of the hens. Mom had spent the last several years building up her flock. At supper, Mom described how she had witnessed Charley kill another one of her chickens. Dad got up and left the table.

He returned with the .22-caliber rifle, handed it to me, and said, "You know what you have to do."

I trembled as I took the rifle and walked outside. My legs were rubbery as I stalked Charley. I found him in his favorite spot, in front of the barn. He was sitting up on his back haunches with his head cocked to one side, as he looked at me. I pulled the trigger and put a bullet in his brain. I staggered back to the house, emotions flooding my body. I handed the gun to Dad and yelled at him, my voice filled with rage, "IF I EVER SEE ANOTHER CHICKEN FEASTING ON STRAWBERRIES IN OUR STRAWBERRY PATCH, THERE WILL BE CHICKEN SOUP FOR DINNER."

Later that summer, while we were away from home, Dad would have Trixy shot by a neighbor. He said it was for the best. It was over.

My experience with pets was extremely traumatic. In addition to the dogs, lamb, and a rabbit, I had at least six cats die unfortunate deaths. I never wanted to go through such horrible experiences again. I invested all my emotions into my pets, and they kept dying. My sisters were so much older than me that I hardly knew them. My parents were distant and older than average. Larry was my only friend in the area and even he was two years older than me. I realized my support system wasn't going to be my pets or the people around me. My love of machines was the safest place to invest my time and emotions.

CHAPTER 35
MOTORCYCLES AGAIN

Even though the rebuilt Enfield ran and looked great, I rode it as little as possible. I wanted to preserve it to maximize the trade-in value. I drove it once in a while, just enough to keep the dream alive and to keep the battery charged. Cousin Larry had managed to explode the Clinton engine on Big Red. I suspected it was from one-too-many speed modifications. Larry negotiated a deal to buy the Whizzer from Darryl Heimbuck. Darryl had graduated to car ownership and no longer needed it. After a year of Larry's "speed-tuning," the Whizzer also died a premature death.

While working on the D4 in front of the shop, a figure approached on a whisper-quiet motorcycle. It was Larry on a new Honda Super 90. Larry graduated from high school that spring, 1966, and needed some reliable transportation to go to college in the fall. I stopped my chores and strolled over to the new Honda. Shiny black and chrome, it was awesome looking.

"I just got it today," Larry said proudly.

"It's beautiful," I replied. "Are you going to modify it?"

"Not this one, I'm going to leave it stock," he pledged. He started the little motorcycle and purred silently away down the driveway.

Larry's pledge "to leave things stock" carried little weight as a week later an unrecognizable motorcycle screamed into our yard. He had stripped the S90 of any extra weight. The muffler and air cleaner were non-existent. The front fender and taillight were gone. It looked and sounded horrible. Larry proudly announced he could get it up to seventy miles per hour. I thought it would look good in the box of Frankentruck. They could be matching monstrosities headed to the Gehry Museum of Crazy Art!

The motorcycle bug also bit my other cousins. Bradley got a Gilera 200 Super and cousin Scott Ulm, from Ohio, got a Honda 305 Super Hawk. The few moments we had together, we would go riding and feel the wind in our faces.

That year went by so fast. After waiting for all the snow to melt, the farming became compressed into a few months of furious activity. Dad was busy; Mom was busy; I was busy. Money was better but still tight. We started the year as poor dirt farmers. We ended the year as poor dirt farmers with a massive debt. Our income had exploded but so had our expenses. As fall approached, Dad and I had a conversation. He was financially overextended and needed to start making payments to Case and Schultz Machinery. There was no possibility of financing a motorcycle unless cattle and crop prices rose in the fall. I thought about it and said I would wait until next spring. The new motorcycles would be released soon, and I could get a 1967 model instead of a '66. I couldn't ride much in the winter anyway...

Honda had recently introduced the CB450 Black Bomber, and it was on my wish list. During school study hall, I would spend hours drawing it. The reviews of the Bomber in *Cycle World* were gushing. Priced reasonably and loaded with new technology, the CB450 was Honda's entry into larger displacement motorcycles. The new Hondas marked the beginning of the end for most British motorcycle manufacturers. Honda had invested resources in engineering and manufacturing while the British were still making machines from pre-World War II designs. Many large British manufacturers eventually went extinct, unable to compete with the smaller, faster, more dependable, and less-expensive Japanese imports. In a few years, Triumph would be the only manufacturer to carry the Union Jack.

CHAPTER 36
PROBLEMS BY THE FOOT

The year was rapidly coming to a close. The fall weather had been beautiful. Even though we were busier than ever, we also managed to be more organized than ever. The hay was all baled and stacked in neat rows, the barns were clean, and the Caterpillar equipment was serviced and ready for another year.

Unbeknownst to me at the time, we were living in the *North American Central Flyway,* and it was perfect for hunting. Clouds of waterfowl would darken the skies. Pheasant, ducks, geese, and partridges were abundant. Sandhill cranes and the occasional whooping crane would grace our fields. Herons, pelicans, and seagulls bobbed in the lakes and sloughs. We had hawks, owls, buzzards and golden eagles. Songbirds of every size and type graced our farm.

The weather would usually stay nice until mid-December, with the coldest weather occurring around New Year's Day. This year was no exception.

I stayed with cousins Bradley and Greg, in Bismarck, for the New Year's holiday. New Year's morning, 1967, was one of the coldest on record, forty-five degrees *below* zero. Sane people did not go outside for long periods of time unless equipped with proper clothing. The cold weather hung on for several weeks. The insane people (farmers and ranchers), still needed to feed the cattle and milk the cows.

Rubber overshoes were the typical winter footwear for farmers and ranchers. My parents wore them when attending to the chores. Rubber was a terrific insulator against the cold and was cleanable if soiled. My feet grew so fast, by the time I was in the sixth grade my feet were bigger than my Dad's, so his old shoes no longer fit me. I was left out of the rubber-shoe equation and only had a pair of canvas tennis shoes.

My evening chores took about forty-five minutes of outdoor activity. Before milking, I was required to carry ground oats to the milk cows. Then, while Mom and Dad milked, I would haul bales of hay to the calves and range cattle. It had *warmed* to thirty degrees below zero as I completed my chores and walked into the house.

I took off my shoes and wobbled down our hallway. As I walked, I could hear my feet clanking on the floor. I took a seat on the piano bench and removed my socks. My feet were ghostly white. My toes on both feet were frozen solid! They looked like ice cubes. *This was not good.*

I called for Mom to look at my feet. She was horrified and yelled for Dad. Mom said she needed to rub my feet with snow, while Dad argued they should be soaked in hot water. As my parents discussed a medical treatment plan, my feet began to thaw. An excruciating pain started shooting through my feet.

Because I was born clubfooted, my feet were already super-sensitive. Mom had shown me ink prints of my feet in my baby book. The blobs showed my big toes nearly touching my heel! Until being diagnosed by a podiatrist and given therapy, I had trouble walking as a child. Mom was taught to pull on my feet for an hour a day in an attempt to lengthen the inner foot bones. My feet ached after each session. I had to wear specially crafted shoes with steel inserts to encourage my feet to grow into the proper shape. Once I reached seven, my feet appeared normal but had become super-sensitive to pain. While my sisters went barefoot all summer, I couldn't walk without shoes on my feet, even on a smooth surface. Stepping on the smallest grain of sand would cause pain.

Doctor Mom implemented her frozen-foot remedy by running outside, collecting a pan of snow, and rubbing it all over my feet. I doubt any treatment would have changed the outcome. Within hours my feet had swelled, and the pain was unbearable. In the morning when I awoke, my toes looked like radishes. Unless my parents were planning on sending me to school barefoot, I'd be staying home today.

On the third day, the swelling had started to subside, but my toes were still a mess. They bled and oozed from cracks in my skin. Toenails fell off a few toes, and most of the skin on my feet sloughed off. Several weeks later my feet were healing. I had kept my toes and successfully avoided gangrene. Lucky me! It was apparent I desperately needed footwear superior to tennis shoes to protect my feet while doing chores.

During another trip to Bismarck, Dad spotted "Bunny boots" at the Army Surplus Store. However, they weren't "Bunny boots" at all, but merely the felt liners that were supposed to go inside "Bunny boots." Designed for Arctic use by the military, the thick felt liners made the boots warm in frigid weather. Dad and I, not being versed in the latest Arctic footwear fashion trends, didn't realize the liners were not proper footwear and they weren't designed to be used without the exterior boot. The price fit our budget. Seventy-five cents later, Dad and I were on our way home with a pair of "Bunny boots," size twelve.

I began wearing them for chores and was immediately rewarded with warm feet. I thought it was odd the sole was just a layer of thick felt and not rubber or leather, but who was I to question the military? After several weeks of use, the felt fabric had absorbed urine and manure and was now stained brown instead of the original white. The boots stank like a barn, and I was required to remove them on the porch before going into the house. One night, uncle Hank showed up while we were doing chores. He saw my "Bunny boots" and started laughing. He said, "Where are your boots?"

"What do you mean?" I answered.

"You're wearing the liners for boots. They aren't shoes!" Hank snickered.

Dad, listening to Hank's comments, looked up from his milk pail and said, "I wondered about that..."

I was very embarrassed by Hank's laughing at my shoes. He wasn't the first adult that had ridiculed my footwear. My tattered tennis shoes had been the butt of several, not-funny comments by adults in the past. I already was self-conscious of the poor quality of my clothes and didn't need additional criticisms from relatives.

My face turned red from shame.

"I didn't know," I stammered.

As soon as the weather moderated, the "Bunny boots" went in the burn barrel, along with the rest of our garbage.

CHAPTER 37
TRANSPORTATION CONSTERNATION

We needed a better daily vehicle. Our Studebakers were aging. The gravel roads we traveled had taken their toll. The pickup wasn't in the best condition for driving long distances, and Frankentruck wasn't suitable for traveling cow trails, much less on Interstate. Shirley had married, started a family, and moved four hundred and forty miles away to Minneapolis. If we were going to visit her, we would need reliable transportation.

The year before, Dad's brother-in-law, Ernest Ulm, had driven from Ohio to Bismarck in his new 1966 Buick Electra for a family reunion. Dad had fallen in love with the opulent car and wanted one of his own. While waiting for Mom to finish her shopping at Red Owl, Dad and I went to Fleck's Buick-Oldsmobile-Cadillac to look at new cars. The bedazzled showroom displayed an array of GM's new vehicles, but the best of the bunch was a maroon, Buick Electra 225 equipped with every gizmo and option available. It was luxurious and stunning. Dad was smitten. It was the perfect combination of his favorite color and his favorite brand.

I was coming of age and was aware of more than just motorcycles. In late 1966, Chevy introduced the 1967 Camaro, the Ford Mustang was in its third year of production, and although I liked the Buick, my eye preferred something a little more sporty.

Dad sauntered around the car, coveting its ownership, while a parasitic salesman stalked him from behind. Dad paused at the window sticker and read the bottom number: $4,500. A year earlier, the idea of buying a brand new car was out of the question. After making some real money, Dad had learned to dream. His aspirations rose above the status quo into which he had been born.

Dad coyly asked, "What's the best price?"

The salesman, sensing a big fish on the line, said, "I'll get you the very best deal. Let me talk to the Sales Manager."

Dad was impressed with the sincerity and honesty of the salesman. To him, the salesman talking to his manager could only mean he'd be getting the best deal on the planet! The parasite told Dad, "Stay here and look over the car. I'll be back in a few minutes."

Dad was ordered to stay by the car, but the salesman hadn't placed any restrictions on me. I wandered around the showroom before entering the dealership's shop. In the distance, I noticed the salesman alone by the water cooler, smoking a cigarette. After a few minutes, he threw the butt on the floor, squashed it with the toe of his shiny, wing-tipped shoes, and walked back to my Dad in the showroom. I arrived just as the salesman began to speak.

"Well, my manager said if you can buy today, he could take off five hundred bucks."

I was a gullible, sixteen-year-old farm boy, but even I knew a scam when I saw one. Unless the sales manager had an office near the water cooler, the salesman was lying. He hadn't talked to anyone. Dad, however, was impressed. He could save more than ten percent off the list price if he could close the deal today! Immediate action was required!

We sat down at the salesman's desk.

"Cash or financing?" the salesman asked.

"Financing," Dad replied.

The salesman pushed a stack of forms across the desk. A form labeled "Loans From Others" took the most time to fill out.

"Let me see...," mused Dad, as he began to write. The D8, the D4, Frankentruck, the new Case tractor, the new Case combine, the new Case sickle mower, the new Case digger, the IH dump truck, FmHA, the list continued to grow... Dad finished the forms and pushed them back across the desk.

As the salesman reviewed the list, he whistled under his breath. A look of despair came over his face.

"I'll have to run this by our Finance Manager," he said.

Sensing another ruse, I followed him to a nice walnut-paneled office in an area marked "Administration." On the way, I spotted the Sales Manager's real office. It was dark and had a hand-written note on the door that read, "Back at 3:00."

The Finance Manager gave the forms a quick look, stood up, and followed the salesman to visit with Dad. Unfortunately, the Finance Manager explained, the forms showed a disproportional amount of debt compared to income. Even though Dad based his buying splurge on his optimism for the future, the Finance Manager was forced to base his decision on past financial performance. The maroon Buick wasn't going to be sold today, at least not to us. He then explained that we might qualify for a different model they had in storage, a Buick Skylark. If we wanted to, we could see it in their warehouse across town. As the dejected salesman tried to make small talk driving us to the new location, we all sensed this was a big waste of time.

The Skylark was beautiful. I liked it more than the Electra. It had a bright red exterior, white interior, bucket seats, and a 400ci engine. It was a car I could love. Dad looked it over and said, "No, it's not at all what I want, let's go back to the dealership."

We returned to the dealership in silence.

As we drove home to the farm, Mom and Dad discussed the day. They agreed they both wanted a better car. Our Easter was already scheduled. We would be visiting Shirley and her family in Minnesota, and unless we borrowed a car, the trip was in jeopardy. At next morning's breakfast, Dad announced he was going to visit with his uncle, George Brose, and ask him for a loan. The Electra was still in play. During school that day, I daydreamed about driving the new Buick to Minnesota. I couldn't wait to get home and see the new car.

I got off the bus and ran to the garage. Dad met me at the door with a big smile on his face. I entered the garage, expecting to see a new Buick. Something completely different met my eyes.

What the—?

There before me was a new, two-door, 1967 Chevy Impala. The exterior was Nassau blue with a white painted top and a fastback rear window that sloped into the trunk. A blue, brocade cloth cloaked the interior. It was a nice vehicle, but not what I was expecting. I more closely examined the new car while Dad described his day.

Uncle George wanted to help but not to the tune of $4,500. He loved Chevies and Davis Chevrolet happened to be across the street from Fleck's. The Impala was on the showroom floor and was on sale for $2,800. He told Dad that if he wanted a loan, the Chevy would have to suffice. It did.

The Impala ended up being a great car. A 327ci engine rated at two hundred seventy-five horsepower, combined with a two-speed Powerglide automatic transmission, and power brakes and steering made the Chevy a pleasure to drive. It was *smooooooth*! It also got almost eighteen miles per gallon on our trip to Minnesota, and, the trunk was HUGE! I could lay down in it with my legs fully extended! I grew to love it.

Even though our car problems were fixed, we still needed to make one more purchase before I would be happy. My time had finally come.

CHAPTER 38
NO LONGER A DREAM

The day had arrived. It was mid-April when Dad announced he was ready to buy me the new Honda. I waxed the Royal Enfield, and we loaded it into Frankentruck. It looked terrific in the box of the monster.

We got in the cab, and as I attached my door-rope to a hook bolted to the dash, Dad turned to me and said, "Son, today is your day."

He was in exceptionally high spirits. I think he was proud he was finally making good on his promises. As he smoked another Lucky and fought with the yellow pickup's steering wheel to stay on the road, I closed my eyes to prevent nausea from the optical illusion that we were going to go into the ditch. As we entered Bismarck, I wanted to go directly to Sioux Sporting Goods to buy the motorcycle, but Dad had other plans.

"We need to eat first," Dad informed me. "Let's go to Jack Lyons."

The idea of eating at Jack Lyons erased the initial disappointment of another delay. The little restaurant was a local institution. There were eight stools lined up along a counter and a constant stream of hamburgers frying on the open grill. The smells and atmosphere combined for an exceptional dining experience. The burgers and a glass of milk cost twenty-five cents each. The chocolate milk was served in thick white ceramic mugs and tasted better than when served any other way. We each ordered two burgers with a slice of raw onion, and pickles. This feast was the perfect meal before buying a motorcycle.

Sioux Sporting Goods had relocated to East Broadway. We drove up, and Norman Tietz greeted us. Norm was a motorcycle and snowmobile racing legend. He managed the motorcycle division for the company. He would not have to talk to the water cooler to make us a deal.

"Whatcha got there?" he said, as he eyed the Royal Enfield.

As we unloaded it, I explained I had completely restored it and wished to trade it for a new 305 Scrambler. Norm wanted to take it for a spin, so I went through the steps to start it up, remembering to retard the ignition. It started on the second kick and Norm went chugging off into the distance. He returned with a grin.

"Nice restoration," he said, "I'll give you three hundred fifty dollars on the trade."

That sounded good to me. I would only lose fifty dollars of my investment and had used it for four years. I was happy.

We went inside to conclude the deal. The new scrambler was eight hundred forty-eight dollars. With tax and license, Dad would have to cough up a little more than five hundred dollars in cash to complete the purchase. The paperwork was filled out and signed, and my *brand new* Honda Scrambler 305 was wheeled off the showroom floor and parked outside the dealership doors. I climbed aboard and started the engine. It started easily, and the clutch was smooth and effortless as I clicked it into first gear. I gave the Enfield a parting glance.

As I sped down the road on my new 305, I couldn't help but reminisce over all I'd been through during my ownership of the Enfield. From a box of parts to its final trade, the memories and lessons I had gained with my first real motorcycle were more than I could count. "Whitworth fasteners" had taught me how to deal with frustration (and to keep extra bandages nearby), the painting incidents had educated me about research and planning, and the fire helped erase the effects of the paint debacles and trained me to not sweat the small stuff. All the delays that kept me from obtaining the Honda I had long pined for, disciplined me to have patience and realize that life doesn't always go the way you'd planned.

That patience had paid off, and my blissful ride was the perfect reward. The thrill of driving a motorcycle designed far from the hands of any asylum workers was a feeling like no other. A new chapter of my life had begun.

PHOTO GALLERY

TOP: EXAMPLE PHOTO OF A ROYAL ENFIELD BULLET.

BOTTOM: ORIGINAL 1955 CANADIAN LICENSE PLATE OFF THE ENFIELD WHEN RICHARD BAILEY FOUND IT AT NORTH DAKOTA SURPLUS PROPERTY.

TOP: 1960 KENNEDY VISIT TO BISMARCK, NORTH DAKOTA.
MY DAD'S CAR NOTED IN THE BACKGROUND.

BOTTOM: EXTERIOR, JACK LYONS HAMBURGER STAND.
DOWNTOWN BISMARCK, NORTH DAKOTA. CIRCA 1940.
Photos of photos used courtesy of Magic Photo Art.

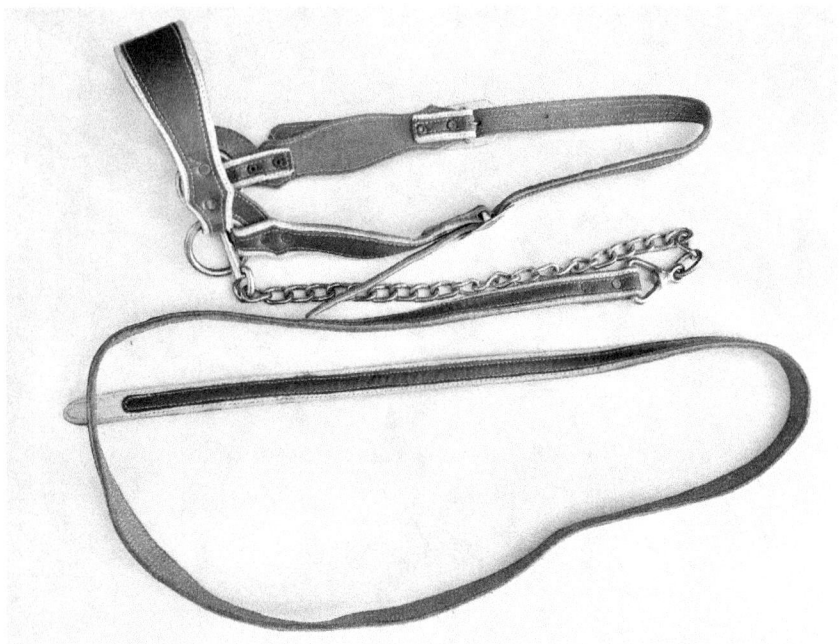

TOP: ROCKY'S HALTER. EXPERTLY CRAFTED BY LELAND BULLER, LARRY BULLER'S BROTHER. 1965.

BOTTOM: 1967 NORTH DAKOTA LICENSE PLATE FROM THE HONDA 305 SCRAMBLER.

4-H CONVENTION, BISMARCK, NORTH DAKOTA 1960
LEFT TO RIGHT: DWIGHT B. HINKEL, UNCLE ORVILLE DECKERT
(OUR 4-H LEADER), AND MARVIN WETZEL.

Photo courtesy the State Historical Society of North Dakota
and the Leo LaLonde photo collection.

For more historical photos depicting topics covered in PUPPIES, LAMBS, BUNNIES & MOTORCYCLES, please visit the State Historical Society of North Dakota's online archives at www.history.nd.gov/.

ACKNOWLEDGEMENTS

Thank you to my amazing wordsmith wife, Sheila, who helped immensely throughout the writing process; my daughter, Breanna, who has been instrumental in publishing this book; and, my daughter, Brittany, who gave me positive writing feedback and our wonderful grandson, Logan.

I also want to thank everyone mentioned in the book. You've all been significant in forming my view of the world.

ABOUT THE AUTHOR

Dwight B. Hinkel is a Business Owner, Licensed Professional Engineer, Father, Grandfather, Teacher, Inventor and 2018 Heart Transplant Recipient. Born and raised in North Dakota during the 1950s and '60s, he hopes to inspire people with this memoir describing his early life and lessons learned on the plains.

www.ingramcontent.com/pod-product-compliance
Lightning Source LLC
LaVergne TN
LVHW051234080426
835513LV00016B/1579